The Religious Dimensions of Advertising

Religion/Culture/Critique
Series editor: Elizabeth A. Castelli

How Hysterical: Identification and Resistance in the Bible and Film
By Erin Runions
(2003)

Connected Places: Region, Pilgrimage, and Geographical Imagination in India
By Anne Feldhaus
(2003)

Representing Religion in World Cinema: Filmmaking, Mythmaking, Culture Making
Edited by S. Brent Plate
(2003)

Derrida's Bible (Reading a Page of Scripture with a Little Help from Derrida)
Edited by Yvonne Sherwood
(2004)

Feminist New Testament Studies: Global and Future Perspectives
Edited by Kathleen O'Brien Wicker, Althea Spencer Miller, and Musa W. Dube
(2005)

Women's Renunciation in South Asia: Nuns, Yoginis, Saints, and Singers
Edited by Meena Khandelwal, Sondra L. Hausner, and Ann Grodzins Gold
(2006)

Retheorizing Religion in Nepal
By Gregory Price Grieve
(2006)

The Religious Dimensions of Advertising
By Tricia Sheffield
(2006)

Gender, Religion, and Culture in the Premodern World
Edited by Brian Britt and Alexandra Cuffel
(2007)

THE RELIGIOUS DIMENSIONS OF ADVERTISING

TRICIA SHEFFIELD

THE RELIGIOUS DIMENSIONS OF ADVERTISING

Permission citation:
Portions of chapter 1 and chapter 3 were first published as a supplementary article entitled "Advertising" by Tricia Sheffield in *Religion and American Cultures: An Encyclopedia of Traditions, Diversity, and Popular Expressions*, Volume 2, edited by Gary Laderman and Luis Leon, Santa Barbara, CA: ABC-CLIO, 2003. Permission granted for use by the publisher. Sections "Policing the Body: Foucault's Theory of the Body as Inscriptive Surface" and "Embodied Subjectivity and the Oppositional Gaze" in chapter 5 were first published in "Cover Girls: Toward a Theory of Female Divine Embodiment," in *The Journal of Religion and Society*, Volume 4, edited by Ronald Simkins, Omaha, Nebraska: Creighton University, 2002.

First published in 2006 by
PALGRAVE MACMILLAN™
175 Fifth Avenue, New York, N.Y. 10010 and
Houndmills, Basingstoke, Hampshire, England RG21 6XS
Companies and representatives throughout the world.

PALGRAVE MACMILLAN is the global academic imprint of the Palgrave Macmillan division of St. Martin's Press, LLC and of Palgrave Macmillan Ltd. Macmillan® is a registered trademark in the United States, United Kingdom and other countries. Palgrave is a registered trademark in the European Union and other countries.

ISBN-13: 978–1–4039–7470–9
ISBN-10: 1–4039–7470–5

Library of Congress Cataloging-in-Publication Data

Sheffield, Tricia.
    The Religious dimensions of advertising / Tricia Sheffield.
        p. cm.—(Religion/culture/critique)
    Includes bibliographical references
    ISBN 1–4039–7470–5 (alk. paper)
        1. Religion in advertising. 2. Consumption (Economics)—Religious aspects. I. Title. II. Series.

HF5821.S49 2006
659.1—dc22   2006043261

A catalogue record for this book is available from the British Library.

Design by Newgen Imaging Systems (P) Ltd., Chennai, India.

First edition: November 2006

10 9 8 7 6 5 4 3 2 1

Printed in the United States of America.

For my grandmother,
Hazel Gregg

Contents

Series Editor's Preface

RELIGION/CULTURE/CRITIQUE is a series devoted to publishing work that addresses religion's centrality to a wide range of settings and debates, both contemporary and historical, and that critically engages the category of "religion" itself. This series is conceived as a place where readers will be invited to explore how "religion"—whether embedded in texts, practices, communities, or ideologies—intersects with social and political interests, institutions, and identities.

In a 1921 fragment, "Capitalism as Religion," Walter Benjamin engaged in a brief and provocative thought-experiment aimed at understanding the ascendancy of capitalism as a system of conviction and ritual practice. Using the category of "religion" as an interpretive wedge, Benjamin sought to cast new light on the burgeoning economic system that would, in the next decades, radically transform virtually every dimension of social life around the globe in ways that he could only have partially glimpsed or anticipated. As its title suggests, *The Religious Dimensions of Advertising* focuses on one dimension of the story of religion and/as capitalism—advertising, that quintessential creator and mobilizer of desire. Approaching the question of advertising's religious character through a critical theological method, author Tricia Sheffield challenges readers to think anew about materiality, representation, meaning-production, value, and the ritualized everyday. Classical theories of religion meet cultural analysis and ethically inflected theological method in this book. Neither "advertising" nor "religion" will ever look quite the same after one has traveled through Sheffield's reading of their intersections. *The Religious Dimensions of Advertising* makes a salutary contribution to the theoretical discussions that the RELIGION/ CULTURE/CRITIQUE series hopes to stage and encourage.

Elizabeth A. Castelli
RELIGION/CULTURE/CRITIQUE SERIES EDITOR

New York City
March 2006

Preface

I remember my sister sitting me down the summer before my first year of high school and having a talk with me about "dress code." She stated that I could no longer wear my generic jeans, Jack Daniels liquor T-shirts, or leather surfer sandals. If I wanted to be a part of and admired by the "in crowd," I needed to have the correct style (in this case, "preppy"), which would win me their appreciation. Thus, taking her advice seriously, because most fourteen-year-old young women want to belong to the elite group at school and win the approval of their older sisters, we went shopping at the local mall, or what Jesuit scholar John Kavanaugh calls the "cathedral of consumption." With my hard-earned summer work money, I bought expensive Ralph Lauren polo shirts, Jack Rogers sandals, Papagallo purses, and Calvin Klein jeans. All of these clothes were emblems of an upper- middle-class life of which we clearly were not a part, but as evidenced by my sister's conversation something she (we?) desired. Our status at school was linked to the objects we possessed and wore on our bodies. Looking back on that time, my new found dress code seemed to afford me with what some might consider a socially active high school career.

This personal narrative is one of the first memories I have of consciously participating in the culture of consumer capitalism. To be sure, I participated, and still do in many other ways, but I remember this incident because it marked a shift to my being valued by what I owned and wore rather than who I was or what I thought. In addition, it was my first cognizant recognition of the construction of my identity as a consumer. Now, after years of work in the areas of religion and cultural studies, I am able to reflect on this value system as one that is based on an ethic of hierarchical consumerism that values people more through their relationships with objects than with other humans. Indeed, in the United States, the culture of consumer capitalism communicates this valuation through "sacralizing" the ownership of objects. And how the culture mediates this relationship is through advertising.

It is my belief that advertising, in the guise of divine mediator and consumer sacrament, helps mediate ultimate concern, which communicates to the individual the objects of value in the culture of consumer capitalism. I propose that advertising is best understood through a totemic lens, in that totems mark a group of people as a specific consumer community. The totem (along with its totemic principle) is an object that acts as a liaison for the divine and society. By transforming objects into symbols of desire through image production, advertising groups individuals into consumption clans insofar as they possess the commodity-totems, and subsequently its image.

The possession of the totemic image is often a location from which individuals produce and perform identity. Advertising designates people as consumption clans through the ownership of commodity-totems, and this designation is often used for collective and social maintenance. How individuals recognize each other is by the totem that a person possesses as a sign of one's participation in the culture of consumer capitalism. The power of advertising resides in its ability not only to target the desires of the individual through commodity-totems, but also to maintain and support these desires in a community accepting these objects as valid and valuable.

The idea for this dissertation-turned-book first occurred to me when I read Sut Jhally's essay, "Advertising as Religion: The Dialectic of Technology and Magic." I was very excited by what Jhally had to say concerning advertising; that is, advertising, in a capitalist society, functions as a religion. He probed further and asked if advertising is indeed a religion, what kind of religion is it? This incisive question seemed to me to be the heart of his argument. But, then the essay abruptly ended by discussing technology and magic, and claiming that advertising was a fetish religion. Yet, he did not seem to explore what I considered to be so fundamental to his thesis; that is, what kind of religion was advertising? Perhaps this was because at the time, I was being trained as a theologian and he is a professor of communications; we simply had a difference of disciplinary focus. The more I thought about his question and subsequent assertion, the greater my desire became for trying to answer that question. I wrote a joint paper in graduate school with my fellow colleague, Ralph Lang, wherein we interrogated Jhally's thesis that advertising was a religion. I proposed the idea to Ralph that I thought advertising was not necessarily a religion, but it did have religious dimensions. I knew then that I wanted the religious dimensions of advertising to be the focus of further graduate work. That essay was the tiny mustard seed that grew into a large tree that took up most of my living and thinking space for the next nine years.

It wasn't until I was introduced to Emile Durkheim's *The Elementary Forms of Religious Life* that the seed began to take shape and actually blossom. I wrote in the front of my copy of *Forms*, "religion is the sacralization of society." I then began to think about what American economic culture sacralizes. What are the current totems in the United States? How are they mediated to individuals? Durkheim states, "The totem is above all a symbol, a tangible expression of something else. But of what?" It was this line of questioning that led me to the current argument that advertising is not after all, a religion, as Jhally states, but advertising has religious dimensions that reflect a totemic discourse.

By combining my fledgling idea that advertising has religious dimensions, with the theories of Durkheim, I knew how I wanted to contest Jhally's assertion that advertising was a fetish religion. This manuscript is an attempt at constructing my argument along with, and sometimes against Jhally, in light of what has been a tenuous relationship with advertising.

As one might expect with any writing project, there are numerous people to thank. All in some way have contributed to watering that tiny mustard seed, which I spoke of earlier. To that end, the production and editorial staff at Palgrave Macmillan, especially Amanda Johnson and Emily Leithauser, has been more than helpful in seeing this book to its completion. I have appreciated their hard work and keen insight throughout the process. A special note of thanks is given to series editor Elizabeth Castelli who believed in this project when it was in its fledgling stages. I am extremely grateful for her continued support in my academic career. Three tireless advocates for this thesis, Mark Taylor, Terry Todd, and Catherine Keller, comprised my dissertation committee. At Princeton Theological Seminary, Mark

introduced me to the concept of interrogating the oppressive structures of sexism, racism, classism, heterosexism, and imperialism as
they are linked with religion. What I learned through Mark has been
a part of my methodology ever since. Terry Todd was a breath of
fresh air for me at Drew, as he and I connected not only on scholarly
interests, but also on similar religious backgrounds. His enthusiasm
then and now for my topic has enabled me to keep researching and
writing. An enormous amount of thanks must go to my advisor,
Catherine Keller, who has indeed embodied the term "tireless
advocate." Catherine was an extremely supportive mediator for this
work, even when it did not fit in with the traditional understanding
of theological and religious studies in the department at Drew
University. After I told her that I did not want to pursue theology
and religion from a confessional standpoint, she allowed me to create
my own interdisciplinary study of religion. She has read, and reread
this manuscript, and given detailed comments, which I believe has
made me a better writer, if not a more concise and coherent teacher.

While thinking about and writing this manuscript, I was given
the extraordinary privilege of teaching at the Institute for Research
on Women and Gender (IRWaG) at Columbia University by my
friend and colleague, Christia Mercer, and subsequently Rosalind
Morris and Lila Abu-Lughod. I have learned so much from the students at Columbia; indeed, their keen minds and challenging questions have shaped and formed this manuscript. To my current and
former students at IRWaG, and to Page Jackson, the assistant to the
administrator at IRWaG who has also been a good friend, a hearty
thanks is imperative.

Many friends have shared the burden of this manuscript by lis-
tening to my thoughts, and seeing my struggle with finding time to
write. A special thanks to the advisees of Catherine Keller for their
critical feedback on earlier drafts of the work. To all the members of
the Monkey Dungeon (and you know who you are), a unique debt
of gratitude is extended. My dearest friend, Diana Benton, deserves
special recognition. Diana has been a source of support and love
throughout this process. When at times I did not want to continue
due to exhaustion (for often we give up life for survival), she admon-
ished me to keep writing and teaching. I hope in some small way I
have been just as encouraging with her opera career.

I grew up in the South, and was raised in the Southern Baptist tradition. My religious upbringing was assuredly very conservative, but my home life did not exactly match this ideology. It was obvious from an early age that the women of my family were the locus of power. For example, my mother once gave me a T-shirt that read, "Anything boys can do, girls can do better." This feminist assertion, of course, did not apply to the religious discourse of conservative Southern Baptists. Nevertheless, my parents, Art Sheffield and Joy Gregg, and sister, Cinda Jones, have been a neverending source of support and encouragement throughout my educational process. It is to my family's credit that they did not listen and take seriously the sexist preaching that was espoused every Sunday from the pulpit, and thus project it onto their daughter and sibling.

I am especially thankful to my mother for admonishing me never to get married, and/or have children, because, as she put it "You have too much to do with your career." Not many women get this liberatory kind of advice from their mothers; often they are told to uphold the "feminine mystique" so as to reproduce "natural" roles of domesticity. Nevertheless, during the research and writing of this book, I did meet a wonderful person to whom I am now married. John has been a source of love, inspiration, safety, and intellectual challenge to my daily lived experiences. His tireless admonishment to "just finish the dissertation" helped me to do just that. John truly is my life partner in so many ways. Not only did I get married, but I also "inherited" the wonderful task of helping to care for John's daughter, Miranda Strand. A deep sense of gratitude must also be extended to Miranda for allowing me to sit at her desk and type the manuscript when I knew she would have much rather been sitting there herself working on her novel, *Pittamayne*. Much of the feminist work that is present in this book and in my teaching is so that she inherits a legacy that sees the end of oppression wrought through dominative structures of normative gender roles.

Finally, throughout the research and writing of this project, my grandmother had been ill with Alzheimer's disease. As I have progressed in my career, I have watched one of the strongest most independent women I know slowly regress into the suffocating cobwebs of her own mind. Without going into the details of her personal history, suffice it to say she often did not fit into the genteel

Southern woman's paradigm. In early 2005, my grandmother was diagnosed with renal failure and Hospice was called in to make her "passing" as comfortable as possible. She died in April 2005, one month after I defended my dissertation. I would like to think that if I had handed this manuscript to her and showed her what I have accomplished, there might be one second of recognition, and possibly another fleeting second of the unconditional love I had become so accustomed to receiving from her throughout the years. I live with the assurance that my grandmother has always loved me and been proud of me. It is with undying admiration that I dedicate this book to an amazing woman, Hazel Gregg.

Introduction

In "Advertising as Religion: The Dialectic of Technology and Magic," Sut Jhally utilizes a Marxian analysis to argue that advertising functions as a fetish religion in late capitalism. This is an illuminating thesis, for inasmuch as scholarship has analyzed the role of advertising in American society, and has affirmed or denied its function as a religion, it is Jhally who poses the qualifying question for the debate: If advertising is a religion, what kind of religion is it?[1] My goal is to turn Jhally's thesis into a question for critical theological studies;[2] that is, for a perspective configured by an engagement with the religious practices of the Christian theological tradition.

Jhally remarks that the concept of fetishism was deployed by nineteenth-century anthropology to designate the first stage of general religious development.[3] A fetish is an object believed to have magical properties and thought to contain the spirit of its creator, or a spirit that will serve some practical, everyday value. He concludes that advertising is akin to a fetish religion, whereby fetishism is not a total spiritual belief system, but rather part of a larger one in which its adherents may have a belief in a higher spiritual power, such as a Supreme Being.[4]

Jhally is not the only scholar to assert that advertising is a type of religion. James Twitchell states, "[I]n a most profound sense, advertising and religion are part of the same meaning-making process. They attempt to breach the gap between us and objects by providing a systematic order *and* a promise of salvation. They deliver the goods."[5] The difference between Jhally and Twitchell, however, is that Jhally views advertising as a negative institution whereby objects are valued over people, and Twitchell claims that advertising points to the positive "natural" human desire to buy and consume.

Jhally's theories raise several questions that are important for theological and religious studies. First, how is he defining the term "religion?" Second, what, or who is the "Supreme Being" in his system? Is it consumerism? Further, how does one distinguish which objects are fetishes? Are there collective rituals in the culture of consumer capitalism by which one comes to know and worship the objects?[6]

One of the ways I answer such questions is by interrogating multiple definitions of religion. Many cultural critics assign religious categories to certain aspects of society without first explaining how they are defining religion. Historian R. Laurence Moore notes that even if one is not necessarily a religious person, to ascribe the property of religion to cultural institutions tends to evoke a peculiar type of significance or value, if not emotional response.[7] Thus, the first part of chapter 1 analyzes varying Western definitions of religion in order to problematize the complexity and richness of religion in American culture.

One of the definitions of religion that is explored is that of the sociologist of religion, Emile Durkheim, who analyzed collective rituals in order to understand the foundation of modern religion. For Durkheim, religion is a social construction by which people constitute themselves into a moral community. In his great work *The Elementary Forms of Religious Life*, he states, "Religion is an eminently social thing. Religious representations are collective representations that express collective realities; rites are ways of acting that are born only in the midst of assembled groups and whose purpose is to evoke, maintain, or recreate certain mental states of these groups."[8]

In his study of religion, Durkheim rejects animism and naturism, in order to posit totemism as the most fundamental and primitive religion. Whereas Jhally holds that religious objects are magical *fetishes*, Durkheim believes these objects to be *totems* that are not inherently sacred. Instead, Durkheim asserts that the *image* that transcends the totems and is created through collective interpretation and representation in a community makes it sacred.

Although Jhally's argument allows us to apply critical anthropological concepts to the contemporary phenomenon of advertising, Durkheim's sociological description of objects as totems is more commensurate with the function of advertising in the culture of consumer capitalism. Thus, a new inquiry concerning the form and nature of culture articulated and expressed by advertising is offered from the position of critical theological studies by drawing upon

Durkheim's theories of religion in *Forms*. I argue that advertising should not be understood as a religion, but as containing religious, that is, totemic dimensions that make it a culturally potent force.[9]

Briefly, let us sketch three such dimensions.[10] First, advertising has the religious dimension of a "divine" mediator figure. The culture of consumer capitalism values humans to the extent that they engage the totems of the culture through participation in the religious belief system, and as they adhere to its religious rites. Yet, how does one know what to consume in order to participate in the rite of consumption? This knowledge, I argue, is disseminated by the spectacle of advertising. Assuredly, many advertisers would assert that they are merely trying to sell a product, but it cannot be denied that one of the ways they try to achieve this "sales goal" is to link a sacral image with the product. Advertising imbues an object with an aura of sacramentality by creating such an image in the actual advertisement. For instance, a Rolex watch is considered a symbol of wealth. When one purchases a Rolex, the image of prestige associated with the watch is consumed by the individual along with the product. Advertising *mediates* the image of the object to the individual, and then he or she has the ability to become a part of a "consumption community" marked by that object. The community then forms a clan (the Rolex clan) linked through the totem and the image given to it by the advertisement. The advertisement mediates the image to the clan, which gives advertising cultural power through its [the clan's] collective understanding of the image. Advertising, then, as a "divine" mediator, is dependent upon the reflective and participatory nature of the collective. Through this relationship, one may discern that advertising creates culture and is also a part of culture.

Second, I argue that advertising as an image producer has a religious dimension of sacramentality akin to transubstantiation.[11] Similar to the elements changing from mere bread and wine to representations of body and blood, the object is then transformed from a product to a symbol that depicts to society the manner in which to participate in the culture of consumer capitalism. Thus, the converted material objects are the totems through which participating clan members are bonded together as demonstrated in the Rolex clan example mentioned above.

Third, advertising can bear what theologian Paul Tillich calls "ultimate concern": "[W]hatever concerns a man [*sic*] ultimately becomes god for him, and conversely, it means that a man can be concerned only about that which is god for him."[12] As stated previously, advertising abstracts from culture, and also participates in the dominant form of culture. It is advertising as a "divine" mediator that communicates to the individual the ultimate concern of the culture of consumer capitalism. This ultimate concern is reflected in advertising's ability to mediate the proposition that the identity that matters most is constructed, in part, by the objects that an individual chooses to own.

What, then, is the ultimate concern of consumerism? Is it a form of "religion?" Could it be one's ability to consume conspicuously? Or is it the reiterative practice of owning goods which creates an identity that is valued by a capitalist system? To be sure, some critics call the culture of consumer capitalism America's new "religion."[13] These scholars accuse consumerism of creating a desire-driven hedonistic milieu in which the performance of consumers at the local "cathedrals of consumption" (shopping malls) identifies them as participants in the "religion." The culture of consumer capitalism may surely reflect a type of ultimate concern in that the "sacred" is found in the object that one buys; indeed, the more one possesses, the greater one has for the ability to participate with the divine of the culture. Through this act of "divine participatory consuming," one may see how the culture of consumer capitalism attempts to replace the role of religion in an individual's life. But I want to resist calling the culture of consumer capitalism a "religion", while recognizing the potentiality that it may have to be distinguished as a "false religion" through its imparting ultimate concern in the fictive practices of identity formation.[14]

Methodology

Using the approach of a critical theological analysis, the religious dimensions of advertising are deconstructed in order to determine what kind of society is being "sacralized" in the United States in the twenty-first century. To what extent does advertising mediate a kind of "ultimate concern" to Americans through sacramental objects? In order to understand the role that advertising plays as an institution in American culture, I analyze the type of advertising that Michael Schudson categorizes as "national consumer goods advertising."[15] Schudson defines it as "[T]he advertising people see most often on television and in national magazines, recall most vividly, and think of most readily when the topic of advertising comes up."[16] This type of advertising has its impact on American attitudes toward products, money, and the "good life."

Along with Durkheim's sociological method, my methodology acknowledges anthropological research as a key to theological studies. In this, I am helped by the constructive theological method of Mark Lewis Taylor.[17] In his book, *Beyond Explanation: Religious Dimensions in Cultural Anthropology*, Taylor traces religious dimensions in anthropological discourse that transcend the usual explanations, methods, and descriptions of the discipline.[18] His goal is to develop a dialogue between anthropologists and theologians without subsuming anthropological concerns under theology, as would be characteristic of religious studies proper. In fact, theologian Katherine Tanner agrees when she states, "It is this postmodern modification of an anthropological notion of culture that holds the greatest promise as a tool for theological study."[19] This postmodern approach allows one to ask which experiences are correctly called "religious," while sustaining the interchange of theology and anthropological discourse.

Finally, a third discipline that informs my methodology is cultural religious history. For this, the perspective of religious historian R. Laurence Moore is utilized. Moore asserts a privileged place for religion because it has often been placed in a "category separate from the general issue of understanding culture."[20] He believes religion is a "construction of human invention," which assumes the social forms of race, class, gender, and politics in various time periods. Thus, my methodology follows Moore's historical analysis as a site to inform critical theological studies while engaging an area of cultural discourse, namely the religious dimensions of advertising. In other words, Moore's perspective helps to engage critical theological studies so that one may "reckon with the strategic cultural forces of religious ideas as they are practiced" in the United States.[21]

The book is organized into five chapters (the fifth seemingly more different and theoretical in its use of feminist discourse as it relates to the production of identity in advertising). Chapter 1, "Totemic Desires," examines Sut Jhally's argument that advertising is a religion by asking how we should position advertising from the vantage point of critical theological studies. Jhally's claim that advertising is a fetish religion is contrasted with Durkheim's theories of totemism, allowing me to argue that advertising has religious dimensions. As will be shown, Jhally seems to want to use fetishistic symbols to describe advertising, but then reverts to Christian or other traditional religious language to suggest its functional value as a mediator of meaning. I agree with Jhally when he argues that advertising works to empty objects of their original meaning through the social transformation and mystification of exchange value. But inasmuch as Jhally wants to demonstrate that advertising functions as a fetish religion, I argue that advertising is not the "religion of use-value," that indeed it is not a religion at all, but is best understood as having religious, or totemic dimensions.

Chapter 2, "Worshiping a Totem: Emile Durkheim's Theories of Religion," is a close reading of Durkheim's analysis of religion in *The Elementary Forms of Religious Life* as his theories disclose their hermeneutical power to illumine the religious dimensions of advertising. Durkheim's theories of religion still serve as a strategic site for religious studies in that they afford scholarship with bits of insight that may be used to demonstrate the religious dimensions of advertising in the culture of consumer capitalism. This chapter argues that Durkheim's concept of totemism can be read as "a body of ideas with explanatory possibilities" for understanding contemporary advertising.[22] For instance, one might ask: what are some of the contemporary totems in American culture? How do individuals in the United States group themselves under a sign by the clothing they choose to wear and the objects they choose to buy? If indeed religion is the sacralization of society as Durkheim seems to assert, what is it in the culture of consumer capitalism that is being made "holy?" Further, how does one know what is sacred? Using Durkheim's theories as a hermeneutical metaphor to understand the role of advertising in the culture of consumer capitalism, this chapter examines very closely his definition of religion, the sacred and profane dichotomy, his description of totemism and the totemic principle, and his discussion of god and society.[23]

In the third chapter, "Locating Religious Dimensions in the History of Advertising," I expose the religious dimensions in the historical background of American advertising, from the end of the nineteenth century to the present. It is imperative that one not interpret the role of advertising in a cultural vacuum. Indeed, there are various economic, sociological, and religious changes that have contributed to the emerging role of advertising as a totemic mediator in the culture of consumer capitalism. With the transformation from an agrarian to an industrial society, North Americans were introduced to unfettered mass consumption. What emerged from this cultural crisis was the "commodity self"; that is, a sense of self that was constructed through the objects consumed.

I delineate the history of advertising into five segments of periodization that reflect the progressive yet cyclical nature of American industrial capitalism: first, 1880–1920; second, 1920–1945; third, 1945–1960; fourth, 1960–1980; and finally, 1980–present. This timeline is used to trace the intersection of the religious dimensions of advertising, introduced in chapter 1, as they are reflected in the shifting history of the culture of consumer capitalism. These segments also show when advertising developed aspects of the totemic principle as outlined in Durkheim's theories of religious discourse.

The main thrust of my argument is found in chapter 4, "The Religious Dimensions of Advertising in the Culture of Consumer Capitalism." Here I analyze the religious dimensions of advertising, namely, divine mediator, sacramentality, and ultimate concern by employing critical theological studies alongside the work of varying theologians of culture, such as John Cobb, Jr., M. Douglas Meeks, Sallie McFague, Mark Lewis Taylor, and Paul Tillich. Comparison of McFague's, Meeks's and Taylor's descriptions of the theological categories of mediator and sacrament, Cobb's analysis of ultimate concern, and Tillich's comments on mediator, sacrament, and ultimate concern help illuminate the religious dimensions of advertising.

The final chapter, "Refusing to be an Advertisement," explores ways of thinking about the politics of cultural identity (and to a degree, religious identity), and the religious dimensions of advertising. An important question is how does advertising as divine mediator, sacramentality, and ultimate concern shape cultural and religious identity? As will be made evident, the conscious or unwitting consumption of the religious dimensions of advertising affects the cultural identity of individuals and influences their understanding of what it means to be religious in the culture of consumer capitalism. I argue that advertising uses the religious dimensions of divine mediator, sacramentality, and ultimate concern to express itself as an immanent cultural institution that reflects social productions of desire. As mentioned above, when an individual purchases a product, he or she is also buying a symbol that marks the person as part of a consumption clan. Yet, by giving identity to an individual through the collective, it also stratifies people into hierarchical clans that use gender, race, class, and sexuality as markers of privilege, and subsequently, oppression. In other words, insofar as advertising bestows identity through the ownership of commodity-totems, it rewards those whose objects/images subtend normative social practices. Advertising, then, maintains the fictive practices of the normative binaries through sacramental symbols.

Advertising, through the religious dimensions of divine mediator, sacramentality, and ultimate concern, maintains the binaries of culture in such a manner that the fiction of a "natural order" is given legitimacy by appeal to the religious. For example, it is natural to be thirsty, or become hungry, but these conditions of nature were shifted into consumer desires as the United States developed as an industrial society. Thus, the need for things became part of the "natural order" and was not recognized as socially constructed. In short, desires became needs and were coded as "God-given." I offer a counternarrative to this ideology, which may be understood as feminist theory conjoining with McFague's ecological economic worldview, Taylor's emancipatory materialism, and Cobb's ideology of sustainability to expose the fiction of constructed identities. My counternarrative argues for *disruptive performative identities* that destabilize the entrenched identity binaries—male/female, black/white, rich/poor, gay/straight—which the culture of consumer capitalism maintains through the religious dimensions of advertising. Through specular discourse and female embodied materialism, disruptive performative identities become a location from which to construct an identity of subjectivity. Individuals become able to reject dominant modes of representation found in advertising, and become subjects of their own identity. In other words, my theory works to destabilize advertising's objectified notion of bodies, and then seeks to construct an area of performative identities that valorizes *all* individual's experiences and aids in a formulation of a counternarrative of embodiment.

Chapter 1

Totemic Desires

Always as a matter of surprise, religion is . . . most interesting where it is least obvious.

—Mark C. Taylor

On Religion

To be sure, what constitutes a religion, or what it means to be religious in the twenty-first century is complex. In the United States, a nation that prides itself on religious tolerance based on the claim of the First Amendment, there is little consensus as to what the categories of "religion" or "religious" mean for individuals. This complexity, in a way, has afforded the United States a rich diversity of faiths.

Likewise, the history of Western scholarship concerning the academic study of religion is vast and varied.[1] A few of the scholars that have illuminated the path toward understanding the nature of religion are Sigmund Freud, Karl Marx, Mircea Eliade, and Clifford Geertz.[2] Each scholar contributes in his unique way to provide subsequent generations with clues and insights to the definition of religion by attempting to explore the nature of religion and its origins. To be sure, there is no one "correct" answer, but there are some consistent patterns in the history of thought concerning religion that will aid in problematizing Jhally's assertion that advertising is a fetish religion. Allow me to briefly sketch some of these theories of the nature of religion.

Both Freud and Marx are widely criticized for having reductionist approaches to the study of religion.[3] This reductionism, however, does not discount the influence that both of these scholars have upon the study of religion. Simply put, for Freud, religion was a neurosis. After constructing his system of psychoanalysis, Freud used his theory as a lens through which to view religion. For him, religious beliefs were mere superstition and thus false. He acknowledged though that many people believed in religion, or a type of Divinity, and accordingly, clung to their beliefs with a tenacious fervor. What puzzled Freud was why people continued to have religious faith when it seemed to him to be so irrational. Daniel Pals states Freud's answer, "Thus, just as sexual repression results in an individual obsessional neurosis, religion, which is practiced widely in the human race, seems to be a 'universal obsessional neurosis.' "[4] Religion, then, is a response to deep emotional conflicts and crises. Freud believed that once science had resolved the issues of conflicts, religion would pass from existence in individuals' lives.

Basing his definition of religion on historical materialism, Marx believed that religion was a form of self-alienation whereby individuals gave the credit due themselves to God.[5] Similar to Freud, for Marx, religion was pure illusion. Pals describes Marx's description of religion as not only "pure illusion" but as "an illusion with most definitely evil consequences. It is the most extreme example of ideology, of a belief system whose chief purpose is simply to provide reasons—excuses, really—for keeping things in society just the way the oppressors like them."[6] Religion, then, is a tool used by the rich to keep the poor in a position of oppression. Conversely, for the poor, it is the opium through which they escape their daily toil and drudgery. In the end, religion is "an illusion that paralyzes and imprisons."[7] Marx concluded that once the oppressive superstructure of capitalist society was eliminated, religion too would be eradicated and people would be able to live more fully without these oppressive illusions.

In contrast to the reductionist approaches of Freud and Marx, historian of religion Mircea Eliade asserted that religion was an independent cultural phenomenon that influenced cultural institutions. Eliade believed the method by which one came to study and understand religion was historical and phenomenological. Using the comparative method, Eliade believed that if one truly wants to know what religion is, one should seek for it in the sacred, and through the lives of the people that one is studying. Using Durkheim's understanding of the sacred and profane, Eliade stated that the role of the sacred, and thus religion, (here more like E.B. Tylor and George Frazer), is to transport one from the mundane world into a more sublime and transcendent one. Again, in the tradition of Durkheim, the permanent aspect of religion is the sacred.

The last definition of religion, for present purposes, is from American anthropologist Clifford Geertz. For him, the way to understand religion, which he believes to be a part of culture, is through the interpretive lens. Geertz asserts that religion and society shape each other.[8] One of Geertz's greatest contributions to anthropology and to the study of religion is his view that all humans exist on three levels of organization: individual personalities, a social system, and a separate cultural system.[9] All three interact with each other, but, for Geertz, religion as a cultural system is defined as

> (1) a system of symbols which acts to (2) establish powerful, pervasive, and long-lasting moods and motivations in men [sic] by (3) formulating conceptions of a general order of existence and (4) clothing these conceptions with such an aura of factuality that (5) the moods and motivations seem uniquely realistic.[10]

In this classic definition, Geertz asserts that religion tries to give answers to the question of the ultimate meaning for human existence. Religion has special status as a cultural system because of its ability to describe and relate to these ultimate concerns. Geertz's central idea is, as Pals concludes, "that religion is always both a world view and an ethos" which affects the individual's life.[11]

As one may discern in our current political and social climate, religion is indeed quite messy because it tends to resist any kind of totalizing definition. Sarah Beckwith has noted about the practice of mysticism in various religions that it [mysticism] "is precisely that which escapes the institutional, linguistic, doctrinal, social, and economic contingencies of an embodied material world."[12] For our purposes, one may claim this definition for religion also. Yet, what is the assumption about embodiment, material, and even the world in this definition? Religious people have often been accused of a longing (implicit in all humanity) to reconnect with the sacred. The sacred, it seems, in modern and postmodern times has disintegrated through what some people call the process of secularization, and has been rendered null and void.

One important issue that must be mentioned in relationship to religion is the interconnectedness of religion, power, and knowledge. In terms of power and knowledge, when a person claims to have spoken with God, on what basis does this person claim this knowledge and/or authority? Grace Jantzen states incisively, "The connection of questions of power to questions of mysticism is obvious as soon as one stops to think of it: a person who was acknowledged to have direct access to God would be in a position to challenge any form of authority, whether doctrinal or political, which she saw as incompatible with the Divine will. It is obvious too that if defining mysticism is a way of defining power, whether institutional or individual, then the question of who counts as a mystic is of immediate importance."[13] Now if we insert "religion" in place of mysticism, accordingly, the intersection of power with gender, race, and class in religion is crucial when one looks at the way certain hierarchies of power have been maintained in the church, synagogue, mosque, and in various other cultural institutions.

Assuredly, many people describe religious experiences as private, subjective, and often intense. Jantzen asks if there is any core to religious experiences for all religions. Does this count as proof of God?[14] Some scholars argue that religion is just another construction of society that is used to order our world into categories of meaning, and that religion manifests itself differently in various times. Those who were the keepers of power in the various religions often were/are the determinants of what gets to be categorized as a religion. As history has shown us, those who were considered heretics or impostors were led to Inquisitions, and subsequently burned at the stake or drowned for either having the wrong religion, or practicing Christianity inappropriately. Often, these were women. All of this is to say that who counts as a religious person and what is considered to be a religion is constantly in flux, being reconstituted through social evolutionary practices. Jantzen clarifies: "No social construction is the property of only one small group; rather, the nature of a social construction is that the definition imposed in the interests of a powerful group in society becomes constitutive of the society as a whole, as part of received knowledge."[15] Make no mistake, religion, in Western society, has often functioned, and still does function, in the controlling interests of powerful groups.

To be sure, all of the above scholars have contributed to shaping the definition and understanding of religion. Accordingly, the academic fields of religious studies and popular culture are influenced by these, and many other definitions. For the purpose of my argument that advertising has religious dimensions, these definitions help to interrogate and complicate Jhally's assertion that advertising is a fetish religion. That is, when Jhally makes such a claim concerning the function of advertising, to which definition of religion is he referring?

In response to the above-mentioned definitions, and as a way to frame Jhally's understanding of religion, I want to claim a Durkheimian view of religion as "an eminently social thing," nuanced by Geertz's analysis of cultural systems as a "world view and ethos," alongside a serious discussion of theological categories, such as "ultimate concern." For Durkheim, religion is not based on a notion of an otherworldly existence, but is a social construction by which people constitute themselves as a "moral community." Religion, then, is defined by the ordering of a community's collective consciousness into a social construction that mirrors back to itself an objective order and "structure of individual consciousness." Religion does not exist as an ontological fact but is a subjective experience causally created by the collective society in a form of objective reality as this projected collective ideal.[16] In no way is my definition meant to be a totalizing discourse that is prescriptive for how others *must* understand religion. Nor does it mean this thesis understands advertising as a totemic religion. But this is the framework within which I work to illuminate the religious dimensions of advertising in the culture of consumer capitalism.

The first step for this analysis is to turn Jhally's declaration into an interrogative statement: Is advertising indeed a religion? And if not, why not? Feminist theologian Katherine Tanner correctly observes that "what is religious is a slippery matter in any case."[17] Advertising might contain some traditional religious aspects, but it does not have a formalized ideology as do some traditional religions. In the sense that advertising binds together certain groups of people through class differences, purchasing power, and brand names into a recognizable community through image, language, ritual, and seemingly supernatural powers, it is very much like a religion. One should not discount the obvious similarities.

Second, it must be noted that traditional religion works very hard at remaining culturally relevant in the lives of its adherents. This relevance is maintained through religion being presented as an institution that is foundational and steadfast. Conversely, advertising depends upon the continued shifting obsolescence of objects in order to allow for more products into the marketplace. An individual may show a certain desire for an object through the purchase of a commodity-totem, but that object is intended to become obsolete in order to allow new totems to mark the individual as a consumer. As Leiss et al. maintain, "Unlike traditional societies where forms of wealth and social success . . . tend to remain the same over long periods, a market society undermines fixed standards."[18] The power of advertising, then, does not lie in its demand for worship;[19] its power lies in its ability to produce an ever-changing gluttony of images that are marketed as fleeting ("Buy now!") and not necessarily steadfast and which work to mediate the ultimate concern of the culture of consumer capitalism. In fact, in the twenty-first century, advertising is American culture, or possibly part of a Geertzian "social system" with the culture of consumer capitalism being the "cultural system."

Last, advertising is not a religion because it borrows icons and images from religion for its power. Advertising, that is, relies on an individual in society to recognize the cultural forms it uses and evokes and with which the individual is already familiar. For example, in a car advertisement, three shiny new cars are lined up on a grassy plain. Out of the sun-filled partly cloudy sky, a gigantic white, male hand points to one of them, indicating to the consumer the preferred choice. This hand, one surmises, is none other than the divine hand of God aiding the consumer with a purchase decision. This advertisement is referencing the traditional understanding of God as white, male, and "up there" in the heavens. Indeed, even if one is not a religious believer, this representation of a deity is easily recognizable by nearly everyone in American culture. Advertising depends on this aspect of recognition, and also juxtaposition, in order to convey its message and sell products. Through a manipulation of symbols and cultural forms, advertising gives an object meaning that "speaks" to the consumer, and also provides a cultural context—in this instance, religion—for the consumer to understand the advertisement's message. At the same time, one should recognize that religion also borrows from culture, and most certainly from the culture of advertising. It becomes hard, then, to determine what came first, religion or culture, or even if one finds origins a relevant topic of interest.[20] One can certainly determine, though, when the institution of advertising came into existence, and the economic and cultural conditions in which it did. To better understand advertising's place in the capitalist structure, let us turn to Karl Marx's economic theories concerning commodities and their social value.

Marx and Commodities: Use-Value and Exchange Value

Advertising deals with objects, which occur in the marketplace as commodities, and also with people, who occur in the same market as producers or consumers, so that the function and effects advertising has in the market concerns both objects and people.[21] In his critique of capitalism, Marx starts significantly with an analysis of commodities as the central part of the capitalist market system. He states, "The wealth of societies in which the capitalist mode of production prevails, presents itself as 'an immense accumulation of commodities' its unit being a single commodity. A commodity is in the first place, an object outside us, a thing that by its properties satisfies human wants of some sorts."[22] Marx distinguishes commodities by analyzing their value. At the beginning of *Capital* he notes two forms of commodities, use-value and exchange value. The use-value of a commodity is obvious in the moment one uses the object. This value cannot be abstracted from the object, but it is also not necessarily inherent in the object at any given moment. Marx argues, "Use-values become a reality only by use or consumption: they also constitute the substance of all wealth, whatever may be the social form of that wealth."[23] Marx calls the second kind of value of commodities, exchange value. He states, "Exchange value, at first sight, presents itself as a quantitative relation, as the proportion in which values in use of one sort are exchanged for those of another sort, a relation constantly changing with time and place."[24] Marx links the contingent connection between these two kinds of values when he says, "In the form of society we are about to consider, they [use-values] are, in addition, the material depositories of exchange value."[25] The exchange value is related to the use-value in that the exchange value of a commodity is reflective of the use-value, but only to a certain extent. The cost of an object reflects the demand, and thus the "usefulness" of such an object.

The use-value of an object is socially determined; it reflects the direct and concrete relationship between people and objects. Furthermore, the use-value of an object is unable to contain additional meaning apart from the immediate use of the object. At the risk of oversimplifying, if one uses a box as a drum, the *only* meaning of this box is "drum." However, if one uses the box later as a chair, its meaning then is not drum anymore, but now becomes chair. In using the box as a chair, one cannot preserve its former meaning as a drum. If one does not use this box at all, it has no meaning in terms of use-value. In this functional way, the meaning and social reality expressed in use-value is concrete, momentary, and inseparable from the use and consumption of commodities. There is no mystery in the use-value of objects because there is no space left for additional meaning.

The exchange value, however, contains an entirely different range of meaning in the relationship between people and objects. Marx claims:

> If we make abstraction from its [the product's] use-value, we make abstraction at the same time from the material elements and shapes that make the product a use-value; we see it no longer as a table, a house, yarn, or other useful thing. Its existence as a material thing is put out of sight. Neither can it any longer be regarded as the product of the labour of the joiner, the mason, the spinner, or of any other kind of productive labor.[26]

In capitalist societies, the process of commodity production is hidden because producers communicate only through the exchange of their products. Commodities appear in the market only as they have monetary value, but they do not give information about the social interactions that took place to produce them. This alienation between people and objects creates a vacuum of meaning concerning the exchange value of an object. Whereas the use-value is an expression of the concrete relation between people and objects, the exchange value alienates people from objects and also from each other. That is, in the culture of consumer capitalism, the exchange value has to be explained because it does not contain enough meaning or information about the object.

The analysis of use-value and exchange value is the groundwork that Marx laid as he tried to relate why "something occurs in the way that goods are produced and exchanged to render invisible the information embedded in goods about the social relations of their production."[27] This led to Marx's theory of the fetishism of commodities. As Jhally states, Marx argued that in the social transformation of an object from use-value to exchange value, the object gets mystified and fetishized. That is, to make a fetish out of an object is

> to invest it with powers it does not have in itself. It is not that we see powers in things which are not present (that would be pure illusion) but that we think that the powers a product does have belong to it directly as a thing, rather than as a result of specific human actions that give it power in the first place.[28]

Jhally notes that for Marx, the fetishism of commodities represents a naturalization of a social process; that is, it gives value to objects when value is really produced by humans in a social system of meaning, namely capitalism.[29] This "naturalization process" "mystifies" an object, not only in the realm of an individual's consciousness, but also becomes embodied in the objects themselves.[30] Marx describes the fetishism of commodities as "a disguise whereby the appearance of things in the marketplace masks the story of who fashioned them, and under what conditions."[31] This is the separation of "creator from consumer" that leaves the void that advertising then fills. Jhally asserts that

> the fetishism of commodities consists in the first place of emptying them [commodities] of meaning, of hiding the real social relations objectified in them through human labour, to make it possible for the imaginary/symbolic relations to be injected into the construction of meaning at a secondary level. Production empties. Advertising fills. The real is hidden by the imaginary.[32]

Jhally traces the history of the word "fetish" in order to explain why Marx chose to use the term fetish to describe this process of cloaked production. Jhally notes that fetish is from a corruption of *feitico*, a Portuguese term used to describe an amulet or charm. Jhally states that Marx's source for the term fetish was taken from the early anthropologist de Brosse. In his work, *Du Culte de dieux fetiches*, de Brosse states that "fetishism is the first stage of general religious development," followed by monotheism as the last stage.[33] De Brosse defines fetish as "anything which people like to select for adoration."[34] And as Jhally notes, the inherent powers of the fetish were a prime reason for worship.[35] After de Brosse, August Comte developed the definition of fetish further when he defined it as the first in a three-stage development of religion, with polytheism second and monotheism as the third. Jhally states that Comte saw fetishism as a necessary stage for the development of religion in which inanimate objects were believed to have souls similar to our own.[36] One of the final definitions of fetish that Jhally describes is offered by the great anthropologist E.B. Tylor.

> Fetishism is seen here as the practice by which objects become the temporary home of some spirit which if worshipped and appeased can have a beneficial influence on the worldly existence of the owner of the fetish. There is nothing intrinsic in the object that qualifies it as a fetish and the imposition of a spirit takes place within a religious (and ritualistic) context by the performance of a priest or fetishman.[37]

Tylor's definition is the one that Jhally uses when he considers the conflation between the "old" fetishisms and the "new" fetishisms of the culture of consumer capitalism. He believes what happens when the two fetishisms meet is "the development of practices representing a blend of old fetishisms with other elements, devised in response to pressures exerted on traditional societies in the twentieth century by market forces operating on a global scale."[38]

Jhally recognizes that the early-nineteenth-century anthropological accounts of fetishism are based on oppressive colonialist practices committed by European men on West African tribes. To be sure, the system of belief labeled as fetishism is complicated by the tyrannical paternalism and racism practiced by the anthropologists and committed against the subaltern.[39] But, as Jhally states, these accounts did stimulate a renewed interest among those scholars who wished to study the origins of religion in new and exciting ways.[40] However, the concept of the fetish has remained problematic in the field of anthropology and other academic disciplines.

Despite its tenuous background, Jhally believes that fetishism still provides the best way to understand the mystification of objects in the culture of consumer capitalism. For him, "symbolic" refers to "the giving of meaning to something that has no meaning separate from this symbolism" and "mystification" is distinguished from symbolism in that the "former seeks to give false meaning to something that already has meaning."[41] In analyzing Marx's fetishism of commodities, Jhally's main goal is to show how mystification is still used in the realm of use-value so that the culture of objects is maintained by a discourse of falsification, namely advertising.[42]

Jhally's Four Stages of Advertising

According to the above Marxist model, Jhally outlines four different chronological stages of advertising as they are reflected in American society. The first stage, the stage of *Idolatry*[43] is the traditional preindustrial society, in which the relationship between people and objects is rooted in the "ethnic" culture. "Objects were given meaning by being integrated within the older forms of cultural life based around family, religion and community."[44] There was no real division between the consumer and the object of consumption in terms of geography or knowledge of production. This was the United States before 1880, when mass consumption had not replaced manufactured goods in the home.

In the second stage, *Iconology*,[45] which characterizes the industrial society, the consumer was separated from the object of consumption; thus, the object's meaning for the consumer was concealed through the process of mass production. The result was a cultural void filled by advertising that gave new meaning to the relationship between people and objects. Advertising began to place objects in a different social context instead of merely giving information about the products. In this stage, what is important was not only how objects functioned but what they represented as a social sign.

This shift into the social context was completed in the third stage, *Narcissism*, by focusing on the consumer as an individual.[46] This stage produced desires for the individual by marketing and reflecting back to the individual a fantasized completion of those desires while subsuming them into collective desires. In other words, individual desires were posited as group desires yet never explicitly marketed as such. The individual was always presented as having some sort of independence from the group in order to develop and maintain these narcissistic desires.

In the final stage, *Totemism*, advertising becomes the substitute for the previous culture and creates the former context of the relationship between people and objects.[47] Advertising gives meaning to objects that have been emptied of their original meaning; in this way, advertising frames the very heart of the relationship between people and objects through products functioning as totems for clan membership. As Jhally asserts, "Through consumption, one has access to a consumption community."[48] In this final totemic stage, Jhally believes that certain aspects from all three previous stages are present.

In these four developmental stages, one may see that advertising has continually tried to mediate meaning to the consumer through the ownership of objects. Jhally notes that in addition to advertising giving meaning, it also makes people feel good about their purchase decisions.[49] Even if the decision-making process seems irrational, advertising provides the consumer with some small sense of justification for the purchase of the object. Thus, for Jhally, "advertising provides meaning where true meaning has been stolen" or reappropriated from the object in the social transformation from use-value to exchange value.[50] Advertising then gives the consumer a pleasurable experience of justification for the purchase of the object. Based on this analysis, we then get to the most arresting of Jhally's claims: "If this function were attributed to an institution in non-capitalist society, we would have no trouble seeing it for what it was—religion."[51]

> Indeed, if the basis of advertising is to make us feel good and it has surrendered any objective basis for this feeling, in what way is it different from religion? Why not also tea leaves, ouija boards, black cats, sounds that go bump in the night? Why not God? All these too can "satisfy" us, can "justify" our choices! Advertising here becomes a secular version of God! When couched in the context of religion, our four-stage developmental model of advertising history takes on new meaning.[52]

For many theologians, Jhally's implied definition of religion would be problematic. He seems to be relating black cats, ghosts, and ouija boards to God. His understanding of religion in this manner would be a bit confusing for many individuals as he claims that any of these choices justify a person's quest for satisfaction. Is religion merely about satisfaction? Is God understood in the traditional faiths of the world as a "satisfaction-giver?" Why then make this desire the basis of religion?

Jhally hesitates before continuing his analysis and asks a further question: If advertising functions as a religion, "What kind of religion is it?"[53] Is it like Hinduism, Christianity, Judaism, Buddhism, Taoism, or Islam?[54] Assuredly, with his definition of religion including black cats and ouija boards the answer must be no. Even though Jhally asserts that we are in the *totemic* stage of society, he confusingly asserts that advertising functions as a *fetish* religion. For Jhally, advertising is not a "total belief system" that calls for loyalty to one transcendent deity (Jhally believes there is an indifference to it),[55] nor does it have a "moral core at its center actualized in ritualized form,"[56] but advertising acts more in the realm of the magical, in the "sphere of the spirits of the air that affect the physical, social and psychological world."[57] Advertising is concerned with everyday activity. Advertising's effects, like a fetish religion, are short term, and concerned with immediate gratification for its possessor.[58]

Jhally seems to want to situate advertising in the "context of religion," but to which religious context is he referring? Furthermore, when Jhally asks, "Why not God?" any theologian, or Christian, Muslim, or Jew may possibly associate "God" with the formalized ideology of their belief system. Conversely, fetishism does not have a God or even gods, but contains spirits that work for "immediate gratification" in the everyday world. It seems to me that Jhally's definition of religion is problematic and imprecise insofar as it explains the cultural function of advertising. I argue that advertising is not a religion, but it certainly contains, and has used, the religious to be culturally powerful by drawing from traditional institutions as a source for providing meaning.

To be sure, many anthropologists have recognized that individuals are constantly seeking to create and/or find meaning in their society. I argue that what has made advertising so powerful throughout the development of the culture of consumer capitalism is not its ability to gratify immediate demands in the everyday world, but its relationship to humanity's search for its "ultimate concern." As Marx asserts, individuals are alienated from each other through the emptying of commodities. The power behind advertising is to breach this gulf and "give us meaning"[59] in a world where individuals are constantly striving to create identity in their social relationships.

> Given the central role of objects in the constitution of human societies, human culture and human meaning, one can provide an answer as to where the power of advertising comes from: it derives not from the ingenuity of advertisers but from the need of meaning . . . Its real ideological role is not to create demand, to affect market share or even to dispose ideology—it is to give us meaning. If it [advertising] is manipulative, it is manipulative with respect to a real need: our need to know the world and to make sense of it, our need to know ourselves.[60]

The manipulative function of advertising is that advertising fills the object with a meaning that the consumer will understand, and also provides a meaningful context for the consumer's life, which makes him or her likely to "listen to" the ad's message. In this way, advertising fulfills a function on both sides of the relationship between people and objects. Advertising makes people and objects compatible by replacing the former nostalgic function of dominant culture and then inserting itself as a part of culture. As Frederic Jameson notes, "So, in postmodern culture, 'culture' has become a product in its own right; the market has become a substitute for itself and fully as much a commodity as any of the items it includes within itself . . ."[61] Advertising is so enmeshed in the culture that one is hard-pressed to imagine a society without it, or to imagine it without a society.

Jhally notes that the interdependent relationship between advertising and culture is reflective of advertising's primary function in the culture of consumer capitalism. That is, advertising provides new meaning where the original meaning or information about the object was lost during the process of mass production. Objects that appear in the capitalist marketplace reveal and conceal as much about their production as advertising allows.[62] As long as a product is not used, Jhally argues, it has no use-value and no meaning for the consumer;

therefore, the potential meaning advertising gives to an object is the only meaning it contains when it enters the marketplace. Capitalist mass production empties objects of their meaning, and the special power of advertising, then, is in its ability to give new meaning to the object. Jhally describes this as the "emptying of the true meaning of goods, and advertising's inserting its meaning into the hollow shell."[63] When a consumer purchases an object, he or she is often purchasing the meaning or image that surrounds a product, which is created by the discourse of advertising. James Twitchell asserts,

> [i]f we craved objects and knew what they meant, there would be no need to add meaning through advertising. We would just gather, use, toss out, or hoard indiscriminately . . . What is clear is that most things in and of themselves do not mean enough. In fact, what we crave may not be objects at all but their meaning.[64]

In one's search to assuage this desire for meaning, William Leiss states that in the culture of consumer capitalism, "where marketing has penetrated every domain of needs and the forms of satisfaction, advertising carries a double-message . . . that one should search diligently and ceaselessly among the product-centered format to satisfy one's needs, and that one should be at least somewhat dissatisfied with what one has or is doing now."[65] An example of this is what Grant McCracken calls the "Diderot Effect."[66] Denis Diderot, an eighteenth-century French philosopher, wrote an essay entitled, "Regrets on Parting with My Old Dressing Gown," in which a friend gives him a beautiful new gown to replace his old, shabbier gown. McCracken states that as Diderot is sitting in his study, all of his old furnishings seem to pale in comparison to the resplendent new gown. After a period of several weeks, Diderot completely replaces all of his old furniture, wall coverings, and bookshelves with new goods. He then finds himself alienated and longing for all of his old objects, for there is no longer any symmetry or harmony with the new gown. All, he says, the work of an "imperious scarlet robe [which] forced everything else to conform to its elegant tone."[67] Even though Diderot did not seek out the new dressing gown, its entrance into his world caused him to find the goods that he already possessed wanting. For him the effect worked in what McCracken calls a "radical mode" instead of a "stabilizing force" for the individual: it transformed his physical world and his experience of himself.[68] Thus the new gown carried with it a meaning that was not located in the object itself, but in the image that surrounded the object. This image transferred itself into a social relationship that caused Diderot's estrangement from himself.

Most anthropologists would agree that individuals have always used objects to convey meaning and to create order in their world. But as Leiss notes, individuals have never related to goods only for their utility, or use-value; there has always been a "symbolic aspect to their interactions," especially in the religious life.[69] But is this symbolic interaction with goods a reflection of a fetish religion, or is it akin to something else? Let us look more closely at Jhally's definition of fetishism and compare it to totemism to see if totemism is not more descriptive of the cultural function of advertising.

Advertising as Religion?

According to Jhally, fetishism is a religion that is individually oriented and operates in the sphere of the magical. Fetishism *as a religion* rarely deals with society as a collective. If one receives an amulet that has been "blessed by the fetishman," it is usually for one's own personal use. The difference between totemism and fetishism is that the ideology of fetishism that Jhally describes is an individual one, whereas a totemic system is based on the individual as he or she is constituted and known through the collective. Recall the Rolex watch example. The advertisement may appeal to the desires of the individual, but it works insofar as it moves the individual into a group through the ownership of the recognizable socially produced image that is linked with the expensive watch. In this way, advertising creates totems through which individuals are known in their consumption clan.

To assert that advertising creates totemic consumption clans does not mean that I discount the alienating practices of the fetishism of commodities. As stated previously, an individual is separated from the modes of production through the fetishism of commodities in the culture of consumer capitalism. Insofar as I argue that advertising is not a *fetish religion*, I recognize that the process of emptying objects of their former meaning and replacing them with the meaning that advertising gives is an act of fetishization in a Marxian sense. As Mark Lewis Taylor claims, "Fetishization is a process of collective/ social alienation from the material realms or modes of production, and so is a part of the collectivization of consumer meaning that totemism implies."[70] Indeed, fetishization is enveloped by totemic forces in the movement from the individual to the collective.

Jhally claims that magic is one of the predominant systems through which advertising focuses its power for meaning-making. He states, "[W]hy does advertising focus so much attention on the use of magic rather than on some other, more spiritual system of beliefs?"[71] Jhally relies on Raymond Williams assertion that "the system of organized magic . . . is modern advertising."[72] Advertising does admittedly create a "magical" opportunity for the individual when it promises an air of "coolness" if a certain product is purchased. However, magic is usually a *device* employed in advertisements, when normally inanimate objects come alive and speak to the consumer. *But magic is not the culture created and sustained by advertising.*[73] It is in the image, or the totemic principle that is created by advertising, and the subsequent desire to be a part of the *culture of consumer capitalism* that makes advertising so powerful. By "branding" objects as commodity-totems, advertising empowers people to belong, to sign themselves as a part of a certain group or generation through the religious dimensions of advertising.

I want to suggest that advertising designates people into consumption clans through the alienation of individuals from the means of production and the subsequent move to ownership of commodity-totems. This designation is often used for collective and social maintenance. How individuals recognize each other is by the totem that one possesses as a sign of one's participation in the culture of consumer capitalism. Judith Williamson views advertising as having totemic principles when she argues in her seminal book *Decoding Advertisements* that

> one reason for my use of the word 'totemism' is that it describes a particular formation of groups which cannot be mistaken for the groups of class difference. Advertisements obscure and avoid the real issues of society, those relating to work: to jobs and wages and who works for whom. They create systems of social differentiation which are a veneer on the basic class structure of our society.[74]

The power of advertising resides in its ability not only to target the desires of the individual through commodity-totems, but also to maintain and support these desires in a community accepting these objects (and consumers) as valid and valuable. To be sure, a person may use an object as a totem and then discard it when it is no longer trendy. But how a person knows that this object is no longer worthy of affection is through planned obsolescence as it is maintained by the discourse of advertising that relates the individual to the collective.

In addition to the individualistic nature and magical aspect of fetishism, Jhally asserts that advertising operates as a fetish religion because objects are imparted value when the real value is produced by human beings. This is certainly true of Marx's fetishism of commodities, but it is not necessarily the case according to the definition of fetishism that Jhally claims earlier. According to Tylor's definition of fetishism, which Jhally seems to be using, fetishism as a religion does not deal with the sacred; it is concerned with gratification in the ordinary, mundane world of its adherents through the use of magic. Advertising assuredly relies on destabilizing the meaning of the sacred (and the profane), but it expects the individual to have a common understanding of the sacred in order to enact power. To say advertising functions as a fetish religion with "no moral core actualized in ritualized form,"[75] and then to state that objects "fulfil a sacred role in secular life"[76] in accordance with "blind faith"[77] is to conflate the language of fetishism with some other kind of religious language. This is not to constrain Jhally into a tight binary of the sacred and the profane, but rather, to interrogate how he is defining religion alongside his cultural claims of advertising's function.

Furthermore, if as Jhally notes, one of the main aspects of religion is to give answers to humanity's search for meaning, his definition of fetishism as a religion does not comply with this standard. According to the discourse of colonial fetishism that he seems to be asserting, it may help "bring rain, cure illnesses, and ward off evil spirits," but fetishism as a religion, does not attempt to address ultimate concerns; instead, it gives temporary satisfaction in the realm of the magical.[78]

Jhally's argument that advertising empties objects of their original meaning through the social transformation and mystification of exchange value is a rich critique that is valuable for my thesis. The fetishism of commodities is certainly implied in the totemic dimensions of advertising. But inasmuch as Jhally asserts that advertising functions as a *fetish religion*, I posit that advertising is not the "religion of use-value" or any religion for that matter, but is best understood as having religious dimensions.

In summary, the culture of consumer capitalism has various commodity-totems that express the desires of the collective. But what are these totems? It will not be one emblem specifically, but a few—technological gadgets, luxurious cars, mansions, fur coats, expensive jewelry, brand name clothes—that represent an ethic of consumerism that mediates the human and object relationship of the culture of consumer capitalism. Indeed, Apple's latest gadgets, the iPod and the iPod Nano, are the hottest totems on the market today.[79] Through these amazing portable devices, individuals are marked as part of the iPod consumption clan with the image created by the cool, hip advertisements of individuals dancing to the rhythm emanating from their musical totem. The iPod and iPod Nano are must-haves in the world of technological advancement, lending their favored status to its owner. As Mark Lewis Taylor states, "The Apple brand of the iPod mini is not itself the totem, but it is integral to the totem, which is the possession of the product, thus having too 'the look,' plugged in, connected with, under the sign of a glossy, metallic, sometimes colored, item with the Apple logo with bite taken out."[80] And so, what sets it off from other MP3 players is the Apple brand thus creating a totemic Apple consumption community.

In addition to defining twenty-first-century totems, I interrogate to what extent advertising satisfies the yearning for the good life through the ownership of these commodity-totems. The answer may be that individuals engage the culture of consumer capitalism by purchasing and owning commodity-totems that are sacralized by the meaning mediated to them through the discourse of advertising.

I have argued that advertising is not a fetish religion; instead, it has religious dimensions that make it socially powerful. One of the ways it is culturally potent is its ability to create identity. In other words, the identity of an individual in the culture of consumer capitalism is often determined more by what he or she consumes rather than by what the person produces. Harvard economist Juliet Schor notes in *The Overspent American* that people drive themselves into debt just so that they may create and maintain an image for themselves that reflects the lifestyle of a certain group or person they admire. Schor states that the collection of brands and things has become one of the primary ways that we express our identity alongside others.[81] She admonishes us to remember, like Marx, that this culture of consumer capitalism was created; it is not natural.[82] And Williamson adds, "But the objects used to differentiate us . . . the objects that create these 'totemic' groups are *not* natural, and not naturally different, although their differences are given a 'natural' status."[83] It has been advertising that has created a world dependent on such "naturalness" in order to perpetuate class inequality and social stratification for its success. The consumption clans may not be natural; indeed, one may argue that it is a form of "false consciousness," but they are very "real" insofar as they create identity through the ownership of objects and maintain oppressive class structures.

As will be shown in chapter 3, the traditional institutions of culture—family, religion, arts, profession—were the original mediators of meaning. In the conversion of society from agrarian to industrial, the possibility of self-definition got lost. The traditional institutions' function of providing meaning was transferred to objects of consumption. A person's position in society, his or her character and image became merged with objects of consumption. Through this transformation, objects became substitutes for the culture that provided "ultimate" meaning, (ultimate concern) as individuals were alienated from the modes of production. Jesuit scholar John Kavanaugh states:

> The unified theme [of consumer society] is that persons do not count, unless they are certain kinds of persons. If they are not endowed with value by power, affluence, productivity, or national interest, they may be sacrificed at the altar of "our way of life." What is "ours," what we possess, what we own and consume has become the ultimate criterion against which we measure all other values. As an ultimate, this criterion is our functional god.[84]

How was the change of an individual's identity from producer to consumer achieved? Indeed, how did advertising invest the possession of objects with such powerful meaning that Kavanaugh is now able to claim that the culture of consumer capitalism has become "our functional god," or America's new "religion?" One answer is that although the social institutions gradually lost their meaning-mediating function, the need for meaning in people's lives did not wane. In the Industrial Revolution, the possibility of owning and consuming inexpensive products grew with mass production. While the importance of the communal institutions declined, consumption as a necessity in capitalism grew more important. Advertising used these developments to substitute the cultural institutions with objects of desire, and then mediated their former meaning to the emptied products. As Jhally notes, advertising mediated meaning for an emptied object while it also took meaning away from the weakened cultural institutions, thereby causing a sense of alienation for the individual. In addition, Jib Fowles states, "For advertising to be at its best, it must be executed by someone situated between the producer and the consumer, able to comprehend both parties so as to translate the offerings of one into the needs of the other."[85] In this way, advertising is the meaning mediator for the ultimate concern of the culture of consumer capitalism. Advertising contains religious dimensions by mediating the meaning providing function from the traditional institutions to sacramental objects, and then mediating the meaning from these objects to the consumer. In order to analyze more carefully advertising's religious dimensions, namely divine mediator, sacramentality, and ultimate concern, let us turn to a more complete analysis of Emile Durkheim's theories of totemism as a hermeneutical site to illuminate the discourse of advertising in the culture of consumer capitalism.

Chapter 2

Worshiping a Totem: Emile Durkheim's Theories of Religion

Thus there is something eternal in religion that is destined to outlive the succession of particular symbols in which religious thought has clothed itself.

—Emile Durkheim

Steven Lukes, in his incisive and exhaustive book *Emile Durkheim: His Life and Work* asks a series of questions that are helpful in understanding the hermeneutical power of Durkheim's theories for illuminating the religious dimensions of advertising.

On the one hand, one seeks to understand: what did Durkheim really mean, how did he see the world, how did his ideas relate to one another and how did they develop, how did they relate to their biographical and historical context, how were they received, what influence did they have and to what criticisms were they subjected, what was it like not to make certain distinctions, not to see certain errors, of fact or of logic, not to know what has subsequently become known? On the other hand, one seeks to assess: *how valuable and how valid are the ideas, to what fruitful insights and explanations do they lead, how do they stand up to analysis and to the evidence, what is their present value?*[1]

No matter how valid one may consider his ideas, there is no disputing that Emile Durkheim's work is fruitful for modern religious discourse.

The son of a rabbi who later became an avowed agnostic, Durkheim was keenly aware of the role that religion played in an individual's life. As such, he sought to determine why religion was such a crucial part in the structure of society. It took him ten years to finish it, but in *The Elementary Forms of Religious Life* we have a rigorous and rich account of what Durkheim believes to be the answer to the problem of the origin of religions. Assuredly, there are many critics of Durkheim's methodology and conclusions;[2] yet, his theories of religion still serve as a strategic site for religious studies in that they afford scholarship with kernels of insight that may be used to demonstrate the religious dimensions of advertising.

Lukes's questions must be kept in mind when one seeks to understand Durkheim's goal in *Forms*. It is important to note that Durkheim's method, ethnography, and conclusions are a bit controversial.[3] Indeed, Lukes asserts that Durkheim's style is "highly polemical and metaphorical." Lukes states:

> These methodological failings are, of course, very serious . . . and they raise the whole question of how his work is to be approached—as a body of explanations, or as a body of ideas with explanatory possibilities . . . Equally certainly, his ideas have had, and continue to have, considerable power to organize, illuminate, and suggest explanations of many features of social life, from suicide and deviance to ritual and religious beliefs.[4]

In this chapter, I argue that Durkheim's theories on totemism should be seen as "a body of ideas with explanatory possibilities" for understanding contemporary advertising and "religious beliefs."[5] For instance, one might ask: What are some contemporary totems? How do people group themselves under a totem by the clothing they choose to wear and the objects they choose to buy? If indeed religion is the sacralization of society as Durkheim seems to assert,[6] what is it in the culture of consumer capitalism that is being made "sacred?" These questions are answered by looking very closely at Durkheim's definition of religion, the sacred and profane dichotomy, his views on totemism and the totemic principle, and his equation of god and society.

It must be noted that though Durkheim's theories and conclusions concerning totemism are considered highly tenuous, they remain alluring. In fact, just defining totemism presents scholarship with problems since there still seems to be no consensus as to what it should represent. Ralph Piddington states that "[T]he term 'totemism' has been applied to a bewildering variety of relationships between human beings and natural species of phenomena. For this reason it is impossible to reach any satisfying definition of totemism, although there have been frequent attempts to do so . . ."[7] Possibly, what is needed is a more nuanced definition of totemism. According to anthropologist Claude Levi-Strauss, ethnographer A.P. Elkin sought to do this when he asserted totemism as a multiplicity of forms, each existing as an irreducible single entity.[8] He advocated for *totemisms*, not just totemism. But Levi-Strauss argues against this theory asserting that Elkin "divides the difficulty *under pretext* of being able to resolve it."[9] It may be that one of the ways forward out of the debate concerning totemism is to allow for a postmodern definition of totemism that is not totalizing and able to withstand and embrace varied meanings. To this end, my analysis is an attempt at constructing such a definition of totemism in relationship to the discourse of advertising.

Durkheim's Definition of Religion

As Robert Bellah notes, Durkheim's methodology stands in the tradition of Rousseau, Saint-Simon, Comte, and Espinas as it is based on "positive science" and the need for order.[10] Although Durkheim is certainly indebted to his predecessors, as his dualistic thinking reflects, his ideas were new, challenging, enigmatic, and innovative. One of Durkheim's major contributions is that he viewed every institution of human life through a social lens. That is, humans are never merely just individuals; they always function in or belong to a group, family, or system. Accordingly, Durkheim believed that society, just like any other object, could be studied as a thing. Social facts were actual things to be observed as in any other part of "nature." For Durkheim, the social is both natural and rational; it exists *sui generis* and has its own nature. Collective life is made of representations, which are really individual representations, since all that society consists of are clusters of individuals acting in groups which in turn give birth to society.[11]

The categories of time, space, genus, and cause are all ideas that are created and maintained by the collective. "Reason, which is none other than the fundamental categories taken together, is vested with an authority that we cannot escape at will."[12] This authority, for Durkheim, is society. This does not mean that there is no original objective status to the categories. There is indeed an origin, and it is society that creates the categories. What he is attempting to do is construct a third way between the empiricist and *a priorist* understanding of the categories. The empiricist believes that the categories are constructed out of human experience whereas the *a priorist* sees the categories as prior to human experience and existing within the human intellect. Durkheim keeps the *a priorist's* two elements of perception mediated by the senses and the categories by stating that this represents the duality of an individual: the person known as the individual and the person as the individual who exists in collective society. This dual self creates a tension within the individual as one tries to be true to the inner voice while obeying the suasive societal voice. Even if one tries to resist society's authoritative sway, one feels conflicted because, as Durkheim observes, one has internalized society's authority within one's self and society seeks to keep the individual within a relegated sphere. This is what Durkheim called mechanical solidarity, whereby the individual conscience is subsumed by the collective conscience. One may recognize this social phenomenon as what is commonly called the "tyranny of the majority."

> Hence society cannot leave the categories up to the free choice of individuals without abandoning itself. Thus, in order to prevent dissidence, society weighs on its members with all its authority. Does a mind seek to free itself from these norms of thought? Society no longer considers this a human mind in the full sense, and treats it accordingly. This is why it is that when we try, even deep down inside, to get away from these fundamental notions, we feel that we are not fully free; something resists us, from inside and outside ourselves.[13]

Durkheim shows that the categories are bestowed not by an innate quality but by the collective through the process of socialization.

> Thus the necessity with which the categories press themselves upon us is not merely the effects of habits whose yoke we could slip with

little effort; nor is that necessity a habit or a physical or metaphysical need, since the categories change with time and place; it is a special sort of moral necessity that is to intellectual life what obligation is to the will.[14]

And so, by studying religion in its most primitive form, Durkheim desires to get underneath these categories since he believes they are themselves the products of religious thought.[15]

Durkheim states at the very beginning of *Forms* that his purpose is to study the simplest and most primitive religion in order to discern the causes on which contemporary religion rests.[16] He asserts it is necessary to start with the most fundamental religion, which for him is Australian aboriginal totemism, because it is through its beliefs and practices that one may see how contemporary religions (specifically, Judaism and Christianity) have developed. Durkheim believes that if one privileges the simplest case over the most convoluted case, one may be able to discover the essential nature of religion stripped of the added layers of history. Durkheim maintains that there must be some fundamental representations and rituals of religion that express what is eternal and human about religion.[17] For him, the only way to discern these representations is to view the causes of religion through a religion that is the least complex.

Durkheim begins his study of what he considers the least complex religion by defining religion and its relating phenomena. The first characteristic of religion that he notes and subsequently eliminates is the "supernatural" or the "mysterious." Durkheim believes this aspect is a later addition to the history of religion since there were time periods in the history of Christianity that were basically devoid of the supernatural. To presuppose the supernatural is to assume that the world operates according to a natural way. But, for Durkheim, this idea seems to contradict what is essential for many religions, and that is the gods' activities seem to be more concerned with the everyday existence of life. Gods are used to explain the waxing and waning of the moon, the growth of vegetation, and the changes of the seasons. Thus, for Durkheim, the idea of "mystery" or the "supernatural" is not a given; it is a concept created by humans. Most importantly, the concept of natural law is a recent addition to the world of science, and as Durkheim maintains, science is originated from religion.[18]

The second definition that Durkheim rejects is the notion of "divinity" or "gods" because he discerns that there are great religions such as Buddhism and Jainism that do not have such a concept.[19] Despite this, many great rituals of religions that do acknowledge a divinity do not necessarily depend on the god for its enactment. Since the concept of divinity is not common to all religions it cannot be a valid part of the definition of religion.

Durkheim works then to construct his own definition of religion whereby he notes the common characteristics that are inherent in all religions. First he states that all religious phenomena fall into two categories: beliefs and rites. He states, "The first are states of opinion and consist of representations; the second are particular modes of action."[20] He then moves into what is probably one of his most distinctive arguments, and indeed one of the most famous dichotomies known in Western culture as the "secularization model":

> Whether simple or complex, all known religious beliefs display a common feature: They presuppose a classification of the real or ideal things that men [sic] conceive of into two classes—two opposite genera—that are widely distinguished by two distinct terms, which the words *sacred* and *profane* translate fairly well. The division of the world into two domains, one containing all that is sacred and the other all that is profane—such is the distinctive trait of religious thought.[21]

For Durkheim, the sacred and profane are absolute categories. Throughout history, humanity has always ordered the world into these two classes. Durkheim argues that the sacred and the profane are strictly opposed to one another and are jealous rivals.[22] If and when the two categories do come into contact with one another, the individual is said to feel a deep disdain. In Durkheim's understanding of religion, the two worlds must never meet. Even though they are mutually dependent upon each other for their power, they are always conceived as though they have nothing in common. He states:

> The sacred thing is, par excellence, that which the profane must not and cannot touch with impunity. To be sure, this prohibition cannot go so far as to make all communication between the two worlds

impossible, for if the profane could in no way enter into relations with the sacred, the sacred would be of no use.[23]

Thus analyzed, the sacred and profane dichotomy is for Durkheim the first criterion of the definition of religion and yields to the different parts of any religious system.

All of the prohibitions, beliefs, and rites surrounding the sacred and the profane constitute what Durkheim calls a "religion." Yet, he pauses in his argument and admits that the phenomena also point to another system, namely magic. It too has rites, beliefs, myths, dogmas, and ceremonies. But where magic differs from religion is in the way it seems to relish in profaning holy things. Similarly, religion seems to disdain that which may be magic. More importantly for Durkheim is that religion is always centered on a definite group. That is, religion comes from society's recognized collective representations of the sacred and profane made manifest in a moral community that he calls a "Church." He states, "A society whose members are united because they imagine the sacred world and its relations with the profane world in the same way, and because they translate this common representation into identical practices, is what is called a Church. In history we do not find religion without Church."[24]

Magic, on the other hand, does not have the moral community of Church. It works on an individual basis; it has a clientele that may be totally unaware of any other person involved in magical practice.[25] So, because magic does not have a community, it cannot be a religion. With magic thus eliminated from contention with religious phenomena, Durkheim concludes with his definition of religion:

A religion is a unified system of beliefs and practices relative to sacred things, that is to say, things set apart and forbidden—beliefs and practices which unite into one single moral community called a Church, all those who adhere to them.[26]

Since the idea of religion is inseparable from the idea of a Church, that is, a community, Durkheim asserts that "religion must be an eminently social thing."[27]

What exactly does Durkheim mean when he designates the moral community as a "Church?" Assuredly, Durkheim's use of the term "Church" seems to have Christian overtones. But Durkheim resists such a strict Christian understanding of "Church" by qualifying his use of "Church" as sometimes being "narrowly national," and at other times "encompassing an entire people . . . [or] only a fraction."[28] He believes that whenever one views the religious life, "it has a definite group as its basis."[29] Indeed, he even relates "Church" to private cults, such as the family or corporation, because they too satisfy his definition of group cohesion. Durkheim states, "For the name of Church ordinarily applies only to a group whose common beliefs refer to a sphere of specialized things."[30]

Durkheim's sacred and profane dichotomy and its relationship to his definition of religion reflects a precarious imbalance and one that has been problematized by both W.S.F. Pickering and Gianfranco Poggi.[31] In fact, Pickering asserts that it is not a true duality because of this imbalance. He notes that Durkheim tends to favor the sacred over the profane, and that the profane is a "residual category."[32] How then can a residuum be part of a binary system? This would be an impossible duality since there is no parity and symmetry. Pickering states that the sacred and profane are of contrasting status and should be of comparable status.

Likewise, Poggi believes that Durkheim collapses the two categories by enveloping the profane in the sacred; thus, the sacred is assigned a higher priority over the profane.[33] That is, Durkheim declares that a religion is a system of beliefs that concerns sacred things, but Poggi wants to argue that what Durkheim seems to miss, or does not completely develop is that religion also concerns things that are profane. It is both of these categories that constitute a religion. Poggi states:

> If so, then religion is not exclusively a set of institutions attending, so to speak, to the sacred half of the universe. In the very moment in which it posits that duality, in order to inscribe itself within that half, it represents, classifies, orders the whole: both that half itself and the other, profane half.[34]

In addition, religious studies scholar Colleen McDannell notes American Christians have repeatedly "scrambled" the sacred and the profane in the material dimensions of religious life.[35] She believes the two categories are products of the academy and the secularization model of the West, and not necessarily of the people who practice religion. In other words, there has been a false ideal of the sacred and the profane, given power by Durkheim and his followers, such as Eliade, and this privileging of the duality has prevented scholarship in the United States from understanding the nature of religion as it is relevant in people's lives. McDannell uses the doctrine of the Incarnation and its development in church history to assert that religion is not so neatly categorized; sometimes, it is quite messy.[36]

Religion thus defined, Durkheim sets out to discover the most elementary religion. He notes that scholars have considered two opposing solutions—animism and naturism—as the answer to the problem of the most elemental religion. But no one has been able to decide which theory is the primary religion and the other the secondary, or derivative religion. Durkheim acknowledges the possibility of a combination of the two in order to form a *tertium quid*. Despite this allowance, Durkheim declares that animism and naturism are actually derivative forms of totemism, which he pronounces the most elementary religion.

Totemism

Durkheim begins his analysis of the theory of totemism by briefly tracing its historical background. He states that interest in totemism as a theory of religion first appeared in the late eighteenth century, mostly as an American institution. It then continued on as an object of study through such scholars as James Ferguson McLennan, Lewis Henry Morgan, Lorimer Fison, Alfred Howitt, James George Frazer, William Robertson Smith, and Sir Baldwin Spencer and Francis James Gillen.[37] Durkheim notes that McLennan was the first to connect totemism with general human history. Indeed, Durkheim asserts that aspects of totemism could be found in more advanced religions.[38] Durkheim shows how Frazer saw totemism as a legal and religious organization, but kept the definition relegated to the descriptive sphere. Most theorists described totemism as merely plant and animal worship, and did not explore its ramifications for more advanced religious groups. Even though Durkheim takes time to elaborate each individual's contribution to the study of totemism, it is Spencer and Gillen's ethnographic study of the interior of Australia and the indigenous people's totemism with which he is most concerned.[39] It is through Spencer and Gillen's "anthropological" work that Durkheim argues that totemism is the most elementary form of religion.

According to Durkheim's analysis of Spencer and Gillen's studies, Australian tribes group themselves into what is called a "clan." A clan is the most important aspect of collective and individual life in that it [the clan] is grouped according to a totem that unites them through a special bond as kinspeople. The totem may be a species of things, such as a plant, animal, or a celestial being. The clan is known collectively and individually through their totem. The totem is acquired by the individual in three different ways: either through the mother, the father, or through a mystical ancestor at the time and place of conception.[40]

Durkheim states that a totem is not merely a name, but it is an emblem under which the clan and its members unite.[41] The members of the clan not only put their totemic sign on things they possess, but they also wear the sign on their bodies so that it is inscripted onto their very being.[42] Durkheim suggests that totems are not merely signs by which a community is organized, but totems also serve a religious purpose as they are used in mystical ceremonies and rites of passage. In fact, he notes that "things are classified as sacred and profane by reference to the totem."[43]

Each clan has *churingas*, which are bits of wood or polished stone upon which the clan engraves the sign of the totem.[44] The *churingas* are considered to be very sacred and are kept hidden away from women and uninitiated young men. What makes the *churingas* so sacred is that they bear the totemic emblem of the clan and are not a part of the profane world. It is the mark, and only the mark of the clan that confers sacredness on it. So, it is not necessarily the object itself that has sacredness, but it is the image on the object that is deemed sacred and thus gives it the status and power for the group.

But Durkheim notes the images are not the only sacred things; the actual beings themselves are also objects of worship for the members of the clan.[45] For instance, the kangaroo is sacred, as well as the qualities and properties of "kangarooness" that transcend the actual animal. However, Durkheim makes an important distinction between totems as objects of worship, such as the plants and animals, and the totemic emblem of the *churinga*. Since the totemic plants and animals are a part of everyday life, they live on what may be called profane ground.[46] But the *churinga*, the emblem, is kept hidden away and "dwells" mostly on sacred ground. For Durkheim, "the images of the totemic being are more sacred than the totemic being itself"[47] and "[t]he representations of the totem are more efficacious than the totem itself."[48] This sacredness extends partly to the members of the clan because the individual believes that he or she participates as both human and as an animal or plant of the sacred totemic species.[49]

This idea of the sacredness of plant or animal, individuals, and the totemic emblem constitutes for Durkheim a cosmology and a model for social classification. What makes this cosmology coherent and subsequently religious is its moral character.

> By their joining, then, the people of the clan and the things classified in it form a unified system, with all its parts allied and vibrating sympathetically. This organization, which might at first have seemed to us purely logical, is moral at the same time. The same principle both animates and makes it cohere: That principle is the totem.[50]

Durkheim asserts that the totem, the clan members, and the emblem all participate in the same manner in the religion of totemism. Everything in this community or system "vibrates" with the essence of the totem. Yet, this vibration is not about the actual totem, it is about what the totem represents to the people who are called by its name and who wear its emblem. This representative aspect is the true power of the totem.

But what are the origins of such beliefs? Surely, the most elementary form of the religious life is not a religion of plants and animals? Durkheim does not believe it is, but rather it is a religion of "an anonymous or impersonal force that is identifiable in each of these beings, but identical to none of them."[51] Durkheim states, "Taking the word 'god' in a very broad sense, one could say that it [force] is the god that each totemic cult worships. But it is an impersonal god, without name, without history, immanent in the world, diffused in a numberless multitude of things."[52] The totemic principle is a force that is real, personal, and moral, and for Durkheim a force that is easily understood as "divinity proper."[53] Yet, Durkheim sought to discover how it is that such a belief about force would arise. From where would this idea come? And it is in this analysis that we arrive at one of the most contested aspects of Durkheim's theories of religion where he argues that god and society are one and the same.

The God/Society Equation

Durkheim asserts that totemism explains the force that is present in animals and plants as a quasi-divine principle. But he notes that it is not the thing itself that elicits totemic rites and belief, but the emotions attached to the symbolic representations of the plant or animal that carries the allegiance. For Durkheim, it is in the "totemic emblems and symbols of all kinds that possess the greatest sanctity" and in which the religious source is found.[54] But what is the totem a symbol of for the clan? What is the "transcendent" aspect to which the object is pointing? Durkheim's answer must be quoted at length, for it illumines the way toward using his theories as a discourse for the religious dimensions of advertising.

> It follows from the same analysis that the totem expresses and symbolizes two different kinds of things. From one point of view, it is the outward and visible form of what I have called the totemic principle or god; and from another, it is also the symbol of a particular society that is called the clan. It is the flag of the clan, the sign by which each clan is distinguished from the others, the visible mark of its distinctiveness, and a mark that is borne by everything that in any way belongs to the clan: men, animals, and things. Thus, if the totem is the symbol of both the god and the society, is this not because the god and the society are one and the same? How could the emblem of the group have taken the form of that quasi-divinity if the group and the divinity were two distinct realities? Thus the god of the clan, the totemic principle, can be none other the clan itself, but the clan transfigured and imagined in the physical form of the plant or animal that serves as totem.[55]

The statement that god and society are one and the same seems controversial and has been a subject of much scholarly debate. Did Durkheim truly intend to say that god and society are equal within the religion of totemism? Pickering believes not.

Now what Durkheim does not do is to say that divinity and society (the collectivity, the clan) are *alternative* means of expressing each other symbolically. Rather, one is a reality and the other a symbolic form of it. It is a one-way process. The reality is society and God the symbolic (figurative, transfigures, hypostasized) expression of it.[56]

So, as Pickering reads Durkheim, god and society are inextricably meshed and interconnected, but they are not equal. What Durkheim seems to be more concerned with is describing aspects of society as they are able to produce the concept of god.

Durkheim believes the transfiguration of the clan to a form of deity is possible due to the nature of society: "A society is to its members what a god is to its faithful."[57] That is, society is larger in nature than that of the individual; it has its own life force that becomes independent of the individual. True, society consists of individuals, but it can only achieve its goals through the cooperation of individuals as it makes the individual adhere to its program through mechanical solidarity. Durkheim asserts that it is the moral force behind society, not necessarily the physical aspect, which commands the individual's respect and obedience.[58]

> Society requires us to make ourselves its servants, forgetful of our own interests. And it subjects us to all sorts of restraints, privations, and sacrifices without which social life would be impossible. And so, at every instant, we must submit to rules of action and thought that we have neither made nor wanted and that sometimes are contrary to our inclinations and to our most basic instincts.[59]

Since society has this kind of suasive power, Durkheim believes it seems natural that an individual would imagine there is a power external to him or her. Over time, this external power becomes transfigured through frequent social interactions. This is what Durkheim calls periods of general or "collective effervescence." It is in these frenetic times of heightened emotion, in between the normal times of economic activity, that a person feels a stimulation of energies. He states concerning collective effervescence, "People live differently and more intensely than in normal times."[60] Through these times of regularity peppered by effervescence, the individual comes to intuit two distinct mental states, and two different kinds of reality. These two states are thus characterized by the duality of the profane and the sacred.[61]

Durkheim makes this assertion about the two mental states because he strongly believes in the role that symbols have for individuals. For him, "society never stops creating new sacred things," and ideas.[62] Durkheim understood that the feelings one has for an object are quickly transmuted onto the object and transformed into a symbol. It is the symbol that one loves and is grateful to, not the thing.[63] Durkheim uses the example of a soldier dying for his flag. The flag represents his country, but in reality is just a piece of cloth. The soldier's country will not be lost if the soldier does not bring back that one flag, but the soldier feels as if it might. For Durkheim, the totem is the flag of the clan, so the clan member who worships the totem, in fact, worships the clan (society).[64]

The force that one feels behind this loyalty or worship is the force of the totem, or the visible body of the god of the clan. It is through this assertion that Durkheim answers some of his own previous objections to animism and naturism. In these systems, he argued that something as important as religion could not be based on mere hallucinations as animism and naturism seemed to be. Through his reasoning, he believes his understanding of totemism as the most elementary religion answers this problem.

> Religion ceases to be an inexplicable hallucination of some sort and gains a foothold in reality. Indeed, we can say that the faithful are not mistaken when they believe in the existence of a moral power to which they are subject and from which they receive what is best in themselves. That power exists and it is society . . . That exaltation is real and really is the product of forces outside of and superior to the individual.[65]

Religion, then, is a system of ideas and symbols around which members of a society group themselves and through which these members have intimate social interactions with one another. One recognizes that there is something greater than the individual, something that transcends the individual and with which one communes. For him, this "something greater" is society.[66] Through society, one may see how the totemic principle, or any religion, is impressed on the mind of the individual. The collective inspires in its members the idea of religion, then externalizes that feeling through projection and objectification as a part of reality. To achieve objectification, society fixates on a thing or idea, which eventually imparts sacredness to it. Sacredness is not "predestined to it to the exclusion of others" but is rather part of historical circumstances that act together to produce this sacred object at this particular time and place. As mentioned before, the thing is not intrinsically sacred, the properties of sacredness are added to it through the collective's imparting such qualities. Using this analysis, Durkheim adds significantly, "The world of the religious is not a special aspect of empirical nature: *It is superimposed upon by nature.*"[67]

Totemism and Advertising

Sociologist Peter Berger, in the tradition of Durkheim, names a similar process of collective creation as the externalization, objectification, and internalization of society. Humans create a world by collectively externalizing it. Through time and process, this world and its social structure attain the status of objective reality. But this objectification becomes internalized through socialization and thus becomes a constituent part of the consciousness of the socialized individual.[68] The power of such a society lies not in its "machineries of social control" but in its ability to present and impose itself as a true reality based on an epistemic claim. As Berger acknowledges, society, then, becomes a world that cannot be wished away; once formed, society resides outside the subjective claims of the individual, yet it originates in the collective consciousness of the individual.[69] Through Durkheim's theories and Berger's subsequent analysis, one may see how advertising's ability to "present and superimpose itself" through the use of totemic dimensions renders it as a powerful and suasive cultural force in American society.

How then may one deploy Durkheim's theories of religion as an appropriate hermeneutic in order to analyze the religious dimensions of advertising? One way is his theory that the collective produces sacred things through the impersonal force of society. As mentioned above, Durkheim asserts that society is always producing new sacred things and ideas. This concept is important for understanding advertising and its ability to create ever-evolving images for an object so that people will want to possess the item. Recall that advertising relies on people purchasing an object, and subsequently consuming the image that has been created by advertising. As Durkheim asserts, the object itself is not sacred; the community creates the idea of sacredness around the object and thus it becomes sacred. Surely, the culture of consumer capitalism relies on the promotion of individual self-interest, but it does so as the person operates within a group. An advertising campaign will single out the person—"*You* should buy this car!"—but it will do so with approval from society—"Then you will be the envy of your clan!" There is always a fluid motion between the individual and the group on which advertising relies for its power. This is why I argue that totemism, which is characterized by the individual's existence in the collective, is a more adequate lens through which to understand advertising, rather than Jhally's argument that it is a fetish religion, which is characterized by a lone individual who seeks immediate gratification from the fetish (object). Certainly, inasmuch as advertising participates in the fetishism of commodities, advertising works to alienate the individual from the social and the means of production. But advertising then attempts to move the individual back into a "consumption-clan" by admonishing him or her to purchase the totems that will mark the person as a member of a desired clan.

Another manner in which to understand Durkheim's theories of religion as they relate to advertising is through the suasive power of mechanical solidarity as it operates to keep the individual relegated by the collective conscience. As will be shown more clearly in chapter 3, advertising often uses social tactics such as shaming and guilt to persuade a person to buy the "right" kind of product so as not to be ostracized by dominant society. For instance, a woman who did not buy her family the appropriate toothbrush was depicted in an advertisement from the 1930s as an unfit mother whose family lacked that sparkling smile. In fact, the copy read, "Wife Takes Full Blame."[70] It was only through the purchase of *Dr. West's Water-Proofed Toothbrush* that the wife was redeemed and brought back into society as a "good" mother and consumer.

Third, Durkheim's theories of religion are an engaging hermeneutic for the religious dimensions of advertising as seen in the relationship of *churingas* to advertising's use of brand labels and the production of images. As mentioned previously, a *churinga* is an object of the clan engraved with the totemic emblem. Durkheim notes that the image of the totem on the *churinga* is actually more efficacious than the object itself. Similarly, a product may just be an object, such as a purse, but advertising will create an image around the purse by marking it with a brand name or label that makes it desirable for an individual to own and subsequently gain status in society. For example, on a recent episode of the television show *Law and Order*, the detectives in the story were investigating events around a stolen purse. The purse was very expensive, valued at $12,000. When the detectives went to the shop to inquire about the background of the purse and what exactly made it so costly, the salesperson declared that the purse was made to order in Italy, and indeed there was a waiting list to own such an object. One of the detectives commented that it looked like any ordinary purse, at which the salesperson took offense to such a statement. She declared, "It's not just any purse. It's the status that goes with the purse that matters." This example from popular culture demonstrates that the sacred image of the *churinga* (in this case, a purse) is similar to products in the culture of consumer capitalism, which are afforded a type of emblematic sacredness through the image that is produced through advertising. That is, the purse may indeed be just an object, but because advertising has linked a certain kind of status to the purse, it now becomes a desirable item to have that seems to confer a type of sacredness to the individual who has the ability to purchase such an item.

Durkheim, more than a hundred years ago, recognized the ability for things to become sacred through society's collective will and actions. I quote at length the following passage from *Forms* because it aids in seeing the way the culture of consumer capitalism has transformed American lives.

> From the fact that we imagine an object as worthy of being loved and sought after, it does not follow that we should feel stronger. Energies greater than those at our disposal must come from the object, and, more than that, *we must have some means of making them enter into us and blend into our inner life*. To achieve this, it is not enough that we think about them; it is indispensable that we place ourselves under their influence, that we turn ourselves in the direction from which we can best feel that influence. In short, we must act [consume?]; and so

we must repeat the necessary acts as often as is necessary to renew their effects.[71]

Durkheim's understanding of the individual acting to create sacred objects by putting himself or herself under the direction of the clan serves as an excellent lens through which to view the religious dimensions of advertising. That is, advertising functions in such a way that it is dependent upon individuals being subsumed by the group. It is in this way that advertising asks "that we turn ourselves in the direction from which we can best feel [its] influence" and "repeat the necessary acts" of consumption in order to embrace the culture of consumer capitalism.

I explore the effects of consumerism in subsequent chapters; namely, the relationship between identity and the totemic community. Specifically, is the totemic community created by advertising, in effect, a "chimerical" community? This is not to assert that the dominative structures wrought by advertising in the culture of consumer capitalism are not "real." Indeed, oppression is all too present for those who live under such a system. But the question remains: Is the consumption clan a "true" community, or does it promote a type of "false consciousness" through the alienation of individuals in the fetishism of commodities? As Schudson asks, "Is there any community of consumption? And if there is, what kind of community is it?"[72] I agree with Schudson when he answers that "it does not establish any kind of community a person could put much stock in."[73] In this false consumption community, people seem to be valued as sacred more by the items they choose to consume and less by who they are. If this is the case, this is a tenuous and fickle location from which to construct an identity.[74] This is because advertising draws from traditional institutions, such as religion, which often depends on essentialized notions of gender, race, class, and sexuality as constructed through a God-given "natural order." To be sure, many people find this type of identity oppressive, if not false.

As Poggi notes, "Durkheim sought repeatedly to determine what content a modern religion could take, and, more specifically, what aspect of reality it would invest with sacred quality."[75] Durkheim's theories of religion, along with the power advertising has to create symbols that one loves, fears, and respects is a rich starting point from which to understand the religious dimensions of advertising.

But how did advertising become so culturally potent as a producer of sacred symbols, or more precisely, commodity-totems? In order to answer this question, let us now sketch the historical background of advertising through the rise of the culture of consumer capitalism in the United States. In making this sketch, let us trace the development of the religious dimensions of advertising, namely, those of divine mediator, sacramentality, and ultimate concern, as they participate in the offering of totems for worship and adoration.

Chapter 3

Locating Religious Dimensions in the History of Advertising

Whoever has the power to project a vision of the good life and make it prevail has the most decisive power of all.

—William Leach

Americans live in a world where advertisements bombard them incessantly with images of power and the "good life."[1] Since the Industrial Revolution, advertising has reflected the desires of a society that needed more than just facts; it needed hope, love, and security. Many social critics, employing religious language, have described advertising as a kind of "salvific experience," a "system of magical inducements," that replaced the declining traditional institutions at the beginning of the twentieth century.[2] This critique demands that we not view the role of advertising in a cultural vacuum; indeed, there are various economic, sociological, and religious changes that have contributed to the emerging role of advertising as a totemic mediator in the culture of consumer capitalism.[3]

Advertising is a multibillion dollar industry, yet as sociologist Michael Schudson states, there is no conclusive economic proof that it helps to sell a product.[4] Thus, the great debate concerning advertising would seem to be regarding its cultural function. For instance, economist Jerry Kirkpatrick asserts advertising is an institution that expresses and aids a *laissez-faire* capitalism, whereas Jesuit theologian

John Kavanaugh believes it creates a hedonistic milieu in which people are led to desire what they do not need, or to crave objects more for their symbolic connotation than their material function.[5] Advertising has even been accused of being a functional god.[6] In this critique, a person is said to construct his or her identity from the objects that he or she consumes. That is, a person's social being is known by the ownership of transformed material objects as totems of a sacralized consumer culture.

What then are the totems of the culture of consumer capitalism? How does advertising achieve this sacralization process? A Durkheimian analysis reveals that in the culture of consumer capitalism, the sacred is society and the totem. As mentioned in chapter 2, Durkheim says, "If the totem is the symbol of both god and the society, is this not because god and the society are one and the same?"[7] In consumer society, totems are objects to be consumed. The objects are imbued with an image of the sacred by the meaning advertising gives them. Individuals then are recognized by the manner in which their identity is branded by the possession of the totem and how it reflects the image of the culture. And since the totem is transcended by its principle, it is not necessarily the possession of the sacred object but the possession of the image as it is constructed by the discourse of advertising that sacralizes the individual.

Still others have argued that advertising should not be compared to religion. It [advertising] merely seeks to give product information to consumers so they are able to make an informed purchasing decision. The ultimate claim is that humans are rational beings who are able to make choices based on their own volition.[8] In attempting to understand the role of the individual in relationship to advertising, perhaps it is better not to inquire if advertising helps to increase product sales, but to inquire about the form and nature of culture articulated and expressed by advertising in society and how that affects relationships.[9]

In order to enable this cultural inquiry, this chapter researches the historical background of the culture of consumer capitalism in the United States, and its relationship to advertising, from the end of the nineteenth century to the present. Accordingly, American historians of religion have aided me in discovering the manner in which religion and advertising have been conjoined in the United States. Through a cultural and historical analysis, I argue that the "marketplace of culture" uses religious dimensions to convey images of power and "the good life."

The history of advertising is defined by five segments of periodization that reflect the progressive nature of American industrial capitalism:

1. 1880–1920: the rise of the Industrial Revolution. Goods are flooding the market and merchants are seeking ways to distinguish their products from competitors. Because of immigration, it is also a time of suspicion and insecurity, reflected in a decline of American nationhood coupled with U.S. imperial ventures. In addition, this era is characterized by conspicuous consumption practices of the elite.
2. 1920–1945: the golden era of advertising. Advertisers are well respected and lauded by various institutions in culture, yet consumers demand that the advertising industry be regulated by the government. Advertising is considered to be a positive source for the creation of culture, and spending is recognized as a form of patriotism going into World War II.
3. 1945–1960: patriotic spending is carried into the final years of the War, and America sees a return to prosperity. However, the previous suspicions about the honesty and trustworthiness of advertising rise to a new level, and image and lifestyle production (and less copy) becomes the prevalent genre.
4. 1960–1980: the creative revolution in advertising. The use of irony, humor, image-creation, self-effacement, and self-reference becomes the prevailing copy of the advertising industry. The Civil Rights and Feminist movements force advertising to issue reforms.
5. 1980–present: hardly any copy, all image production. Global capitalism as defined by American culture is the standard to which all other economies aspire.

This timeline is used to trace the intersection of the religious dimensions of advertising, introduced in chapter 1, as they are reflected in the shifting history of the culture of consumer capitalism. These advertising segments will also help demonstrate when advertising developed aspects of the totemic principle as outlined in Durkheim's theories of religion. To be sure, Durkheim's theories of totemism are my guiding hermeneutical principle for understanding the religious dimensions of advertising, since it is through the collective, as it shapes the identity of the individual, that totemism and advertising each wield their power.

1880–1920: The Rise of Industrial Capitalism

Historian Jackson Lears describes the "therapeutic ethos" of the late nineteenth century as the era in which consumers' feelings of unrest were precipitated by "urbanization and technological development, the rise of an increasingly interdependent market economy, and the secularization of liberal Protestantism."[10] The advent of modernity became a time of uncertainty which fostered the belief that "real life," as Lears calls it, was something to be desired and achieved, not merely lived. He describes the emotions of society as a

> dread of unreality, a yearning to experience intense "real life" in all its forms . . . they [emotions] energized the spread of the therapeutic ethos, underlay the appeal of much national advertising, and mobilized a market for commodified mass amusements. They formed, in short, the psychological impetus for the rise of the consumer culture.[11]

In addition, William Leach observes that the culture of consumer capitalism was not exclusively produced by the people, but was also partly nonconsensual for two reasons.[12] First, it was created by commercial groups in cooperation with business elites who had as their primary goal the acquisition of expanding capital. Second, in its ordinary business it raised to the forefront only one vision of the good life, while denying the American people access to other ways of envisioning life that might have fostered a better or more true democracy.[13]

Lears argues that advertisers created images that reflected the emerging system of individual prosperity linked to the cultural hegemony of corporate power as they saw it mirrored in society.[14] The power that advertisers recognized and helped create in a burgeoning capitalist society in the United States of the early twentieth century was the carnivalesque discourse and mythic emblem of female abundance as evidenced in farming practices.[15] By carnivalesque, Lears demonstrates how the rise of advertising took place amidst a culture full of snake oil practitioners, confidence men, and charlatans. Advertising embraced all of those forms of entertainment, but it also included religion. Advertisements reflected this whirlwind confluence and "became a carnival of exotic imagery" by merging human and animal forms and blurring the lines between high and low culture.[16] But as individuals became more separated from the production of their labor, the discourse of abundance began to wane. Lears says, "In a disembodied discourse of abundance, enjoyment of the fruits of one's labors became less important than the pursuit of disposable goods. Disembodiment directly affected the carnivalesque dimensions of abundance imagery: they were more sanitized in twentieth century corporate advertising than in the nineteenth century commercial vernacular."[17] This cleansing took the form of bodies being imaged as less rubenesque, more tight, firm and healthy. Unfortunately, since representations of women were the most prevalently used icon in advertising, the "containment of carnival" maintained the image of women as lacking authority. Women became merely "messengers from the gods, but not the gods themselves," and so "The Fashionable Woman" became "Mrs. Consumer."[18] Thus advertising helped to congeal the sexual division of labor through gender roles of normative masculinity and femininity in the early twentieth century

The result of this new consumer society was a picture of the self that had no substance. Gone were the days of American mythic simplicity and honesty, and in its place came a disquieting fragmentation and deceit.[19] What emerged from this culture was "a new type of personality and 'social self' based on individuality,"[20] or what Stuart Ewen calls the "commodity self."[21] With the transformation of America from an agrarian to an industrial society, people were introduced to unfettered mass consumption. The goods that used to be produced at home were now produced in settings that were unfamiliar and whose benefits could not be ascertained by an uneducated shopper. Ewen states, "The claim of the New World was that here basic goods came from no apparent source. The ecology of the land, and the finger-knowledge of home and workshop production, were memories in the process of being annihilated."[22] Lears notes that as Americans moved into the twentieth century, the old way of life faded into urbanization as cultural relativism, the erosion of the extended economic family, and the advent of a new leisure time all entered public and private life. The Victorian code of morals blurred alongside the Christianity of liberal Protestantism as people sought refuge from the bourgeois culture in the popular culture of the day.[23] As traditional institutions—community, religion, school, art, and family—lost their influence, they also left a void of absolutes. The need for meaning grew, and advertisers developed ways in which their products could fill that desire by acting as a mediator between the consumer and the new consumer society.

> In the merging consumer culture, advertisers began speaking to many of the same preoccupations addressed by liberal ministers, psychologists, and other therapeutic ideologues. A dialectic developed between Americans' new emotional needs and advertisers' strategies; each continually reshaped and intensified the other.[24]

However, this therapeutic society did not develop on its own. As Durkheim's theories show us, individuals, operating through the collective, create their society. Society is an internal mechanism that gets externalized as a reified object. Advertising, as part of this produced therapeutic culture, became the mediator for emptied objects as representations of the culture of consumer capitalism.

In this surrounding therapeutic ethos, advertisers were also trying to sell products to the consumer using "the promise of magical self transformation through the ritual of purchase."[25] During the 1880s to 1890s, brand name packaging was introduced and with it the beginning of brand loyalty. As Juliann Sivulka notes, advertisers took a bulk item, such as Proctor & Gamble soap, and scaled down the package and ascribed a personality and product information to it so as to make the item indispensable to one's life.[26] Sometimes the object became alive, a guest in the house to be served and entertained. In this way, early advertising created desire by linking emotional attachment to a brand name that would increase the sales of the item and also create a competitive market. Sivulka states, "The goal was to link together the all-important trademarks and symbols for the brand name with favorable and memorable associations powerful enough to build up desire for the product."[27] Although brand names were beginning to ascribe social status to individuals through the purchase of the items, invidious class distinction had not yet been formalized through advertising.[28] Through the transformative process of branding items, and subsequently, consumer loyalty, goods became sacramental totems of the society. By purchasing commodity-totems, individuals were beginning to form into consumption clans and gain a sense of identity.

Through the advent of brand names, the way was paved for advertisers to use slogans, jingles, paintings, identifying symbols, and personalities all of which mediated to the consumer the importance of the product and established a relationship through which the two could relate. In this manner, advertisers sought to create ways in which the individual would demand the product that had become a "household friend." And in their seeking, advertisers discovered that women, with their minds as "vats of frothy pink irrationality" were the primary purchasers of goods in the nation.[29] With this realization, sex, race and class distinctions in advertising became more numerous and reflected back to society the emerging stratification and thus seemingly "naturalization" of normative domesticity. For example, Lears notes:

> If husbands failed to provide a Laun-dry-ette or an Aetna Life Insurance policy, advertisements implied, their wives would soon degenerate into humpbacked slatterns. If wives overlooked the Puffed Rice or the Pro-Phy-Lac-Tic toothbrush, their children faced malnutrition and pyorrhea. The domestic ideal, long a focal point of Victorian morality, was being redefined to fit the new consumer culture.[30]

Normative domesticity was then coded into a binary of normative femininity and masculinity. This ideology seemed to reflect a God-given "natural order" that was then maintained by images in advertising. Consumer goods, as totems of industrial capitalism, gave individuals identity by subtending normative practices. The image created by advertising was what a person consumed, and this image sustained the fiction of the "natural order" in normative domesticity. Through the therapeutic ethos, individuals were promised "fake liberation through consumption."[31] As American society was shifting rapidly to accommodate the culture of consumer capitalism, advertisers stepped in as mediators between the culture and the objects and instructed individuals that hope and personal fulfillment was achieved through the hegemony of consumption.

By 1910, the worlds of production and consumption, once bound together were separated so that no appearance of hard toil was present on the selling floor. "The selling department is the stage upon which the play is enacted," said one merchant.[32] Consumers became more alienated from the knowledge of how goods were manufactured and by whom, which led to an independent character of consumption. Specifically, one of the predominant ways that the United States became a mass consumer society so quickly was the rise of service to replace Christian stewardship and moral obligation. Service tended to hide the ugly side of capitalism, by placing emphasis on material well-being, luxury, and eroticized consumption. With the new culture of service firmly entrenched, guilt and distress were relieved by this independence.[33]

The outcome was a dawning culture of selfishness, or what Christopher Lasch calls "the culture of narcissism."[34] Advertising, Lasch asserts, played into this feeling of euphoric consumer denial by promoting consumption as a way of life.[35] The culture of consumer capitalism, then, was becoming the predominant way in which individuals were relating to each other, thus reflecting the ultimate concern of the burgeoning industrial society. Early advertisements called attention to the product, but with the advent of department stores and service industries, advertising detected the yearnings for a "better life" and capitalized upon these feelings and desires.[36] Indeed, historian Gary Cross says that the department stores "took on the aura of churches."[37] And as religion scholar Joseph Haroutunian states the "separate world of consumer fantasy began to foster the idea that men and women might become fulfilled humans beings not through spiritual good or through pursuit of the 'eternal' but through acquisition of 'goods' and through the pursuit of the infinity."[38] Assuredly, it is not that advertisers *created* the image of a hollow life that only a product could fill. I don't want to dismiss the autonomy of the individual by proposing a conspiratorial view of advertising that forces a consumer to desire or purchase products that he or she would not normally need. One would not want to be that deterministic; instead, advertising made ideal what was stereotypical by abstracting from conditions that were present in the society. What is true was there was a loss of identity for the individual in relationship to traditional institutions with the boom of the capitalist market.

It was no coincidence that advertisers used ultimate language to describe the "pursuit of the infinity" in the emerging capitalist system. Many of the ad agency executives came from a strong affluent, Protestant background; indeed, many of them were the sons of ministers.[39] As Lears notes, they had

> a faith in inevitable progress, unfolding as if in some accordance with some divine plan. They also had a tendency to cast themselves in a key redemptive role. This was a secular doctrine of postmillennialism— the belief that Christ would return after human beings had created the Kingdom of God on earth.[40]

This white, male Protestant tradition of power was carried through in a longing to live a life of leisure coupled with an ethic of hard work, as this quickly became the American way of life in the new society. When men and women finished their arduous tasks after a long day at work they wanted to find a way to relax. Advertisers pointed the way forward for the individual by promising consumption as a means to achieve that relaxing "bliss." The previous religious longing was now replaced by product desire as individuals were promised the good life through the acquisition of new market products bearing the familiar brand name. The aforementioned desire to live the real life in the United States is summed up best by then-economist Simon Patten, whom Lears calls an unlikely "prophet of abundance": "To have a high standard of life means to enjoy a pleasure intensely and to tire of it quickly."[41]

Advertising was able to produce desire and pleasure through its ever-shifting sales approach. One new such approach after brand name identification was "Reason-Why" copy.[42] This hard-core selling technique gave the consumer reasons why he or she should purchase the product, and worked to overcome any resistance to buying the product. "Reason-Why" gave detailed information about the product and did not necessarily appeal to emotions; instead, it seemed to appeal to reason and the intellect. However, Lears is quick to point out that this was not always the case. Claude Hopkins, a staunch proponent of

"Reason-Why" copy, would often appeal to the individual's emotions:

> Ironically it was not reasonable at all: Hopkins refused to appeal to a buyer's reason by listing a product's qualities; on the contrary he addressed non-rational yearnings by suggesting the ways his client's products would transform the buyer's life.
>
> Hopkins's "Reason Why" pointed advertising away from the product and toward its alleged effects, away from sober information and toward the therapeutic promise of a richer, fuller life.[43]

The "Reason-Why" strategy was very successful, but it soon gave way to what was called "atmospheric advertising" or "impressionistic copy."[44] One of the reasons that "Reason-Why" copy yielded to atmospheric advertising is that "[i]t [Reason-Why] described the product itself instead of extolling the pleasure it would provide the purchaser."[45] Through atmospheric advertising, one can see a beginning shift from the object as desirable to the image attached to the object as the more compelling trait. Objects were not merely things to possess, but they were becoming symbols of status that not only gave one pleasure, but also demonstrated one's position in society and let others know one's relationship, or place with other individuals in accordance with this status.[46]

1920–1940: "Apostles of Modernity"

The pursuit of pleasure was more than realized during the 1920s and 1930s. Before the Great Depression, and subsequently after it, this period in U.S. history may be characterized by prosperity and abundance, along with a certain level of anxiety due to an influx of immigrants. Consumers had been instructed in the ways of brand packaging, and now they took their learning to a different level in that goods were no longer utilitarian items to be purchased, but were symbolic items from which to consume conspicuously. As Cross notes, "Consumption had become a substitute for conversation in a society where rituals of communication were already weak and growing weaker."[47] And advertising gave Americans the language by which to be assimilated into the new technological culture of prosperity.[48] By learning this language, one assumed an identity as consumer. In other words, in order to be in society one had to buy and own goods. It was advertising that gave meaning to the goods, and in this way imparted meaning to the individual.

Historian Roland Marchand notes that "the implicit promises of the ads induce consumers to experience satisfactions they would not have obtained otherwise. By creating a strong expectation of certain subjective satisfactions from a particular brand, and thus inducing a trusting pre-made decision, the advertisement enhances the value of the product to the consumer."[49] In this way, advertising was beginning to function with totemic dimensions. By giving people a commodity through which to unite, such as a new car or vacuum cleaner, individuals were being organized into clans of consumption through which they and others could identify a certain class status. The commodity-totem was given an affluent image through advertising and thus imparted importance to its owner.

Advertising not only imbued the individual with the positive image of the product, but it also used negative shaming and guilt tactics, thus reflecting and producing the anxiety of the age. This kind of copy was called "scare" or "whisper" copy. What was becoming apparent during this era was advertising had started selling certain lifestyles and images and not just products. Certainly the companies wanted to sell items, and advertisers learned the way to do that was to imbue a product with an image or feeling so that people would want to buy the object in order to become a part of the growing bourgeois society and thus become socially acceptable. The object was no longer just a product to purchase, but it had been transformed into a sacramental symbol of the ultimate concern of consumerism that grouped individuals into a collective that signaled to others a pecuniary identity. By 1925, advertisers were spending a billion dollars a year in order to convince the individual to be a part of the new culture of plenty.

As new industries and products emerged, advertisers became strategic educators and promoters of hygiene, dress, lifestyle, and new technology. Ad creators explored strategies to encourage the public to buy more, not because they needed things, but because they wanted to own certain items, use certain products, and adopt certain lifestyles.[50]

It has been posited by Roland Marchand that advertising mirrors society. What exactly were the advertisements of this time period reflecting? Marchand states that the advertising of the 1920s and 1930s acted more like a *tableaux vivant*, or social tableaux, in that advertising was the producer of visual images and parables from which the consumer took his or her cultural cues.[51] In other words, advertising told a story about society by its positioning of products alongside persons and their reaction to each other through the object. But, as Marchand queries, were these advertisements really mirrors for society, or were they more representative of the wishful thinking of advertisers' perceived public desire? Marchand believes that what the advertisers were doing were depicting their own observations of culture and thus showing individuals as they [the individuals] wished themselves to be; that is, one class level higher then they truly were.[52] Judith Williamson notes this phenomenon of "invidious distinction" when she describes advertising's ideology of totemism.

> This means, on one level, that the product "produces" or buys the feeling. But the more subtle level on which the advertisement works is that of "alreadyness," which is where "totemism" becomes a part of ideology: you do not simply buy the product in order to *become* a part of the group it represents; you must feel that you already, naturally, belong to that group and *therefore* you will buy it.[53]

Since individuals believed they already were in a certain class, advertisers targeted this desire and thus helped create a social fantasy. The illusion was that one was indeed a part of the upper class, so one should buy a certain product that reflected this status.

But this "social fantasy" tended to become social reality. In other words, many people did, and still do believe that their identity is constituted by the ownership of certain objects. How women, African Americans, ethnic minorities, the working class, and even the upper class were represented in advertising tended to reify normative gender, race, sexuality, and class distinctions. He says, "But we may also discover situations in which the tableaux, because they sought to relate products to social needs, did graphically reflect central social and cultural dilemmas of the age."[54] In other words, if the tableaux tended to reflect *something* as Marchand argues, what it did was to consistently reconstitute binaries.

What has been purported by Cross as "the ultimate democracy of spending" was truly not.[55] He states, "Consumerism repeatedly and dynamically reinforced democratic principles of participation and equality when new and exciting goods entered the market."[56] Indeed, Cross relates and in fact contradicts his argument that consumerism offered a more democratic ideology of society when he recognizes that advertisements did not address

the needs of laborers, blacks, or ethnic minorities. Advertisers freely admitted that they directed their messages to only the richer two thirds or even half of the population. Advertised goods were often emblems of status, representing the values of bourgeois possessiveness or aristocratic snobbery that had trickled down, through ads, to the insecure and aspiring.[57]

It seems that status and birth were very much relevant in this ultimate democracy. When African Americans were depicted in advertising, if they were at all, it was as servants. The working class was always shown working, never spending any leisure time, and middle-class women were consistently shown in the home, with children, or at least married. If women were not depicted in such a normative manner, they were deemed failures, because they either had body odor or bad breath, all signs of not using the right deodorant or mouthwash.

In addition to these various race and class stereotypes, white women were the primary target for advertisers during this time period. As one adman said, "The proper study of mankind is man, but the proper study of markets is woman."[58] White middle-class women were recognized as those who had the most purchasing power, and admakers sought to woo them in various ways. One such way was appealing to her role as housewife. No longer was the woman, or assuredly wife of the house just "Mrs. Consumer," she was now the "G.P.A.," or "General Purchasing Agent" for her private domain.[59] Just as her husband was the commander of the public sphere, she was considered the CEO, or Chief Executive Officer of her private sphere, and advertisers depicted her as such. For example, since the home had become updated with new appliances, advertisers sought to sell these new products by showing the housewife enjoying her newfound leisure time that these products afforded. Women in ads were encouraged to play golf, sew, visit friends, go to plays or concerts, and spend more time with their children. What is conspicuously absent from these "testimonials," Marchand notes, is just as important as what is mentioned: neither going to the movies, which was very popular among all classes of women at the time, nor having a career is present. Marchand claims, "The wife's expertise and efficiency within the realm of day-to-day consumer decision-making warranted praise, but her ultimate subordination to a higher executive remained unchallenged."[60] What the ads mentioned and also what they left out may have been indicative of white women's desires, and also the boundaries of those desires as portrayed by advertising.[61] But the private sphere is where her power and desires remained.

Another way in which advertisers targeted white women for consumption was to appeal to their emotional vulnerability using the aforementioned scare or whisper copy. Advertising during this era often depicted women as the object of scorn or shame if they had not used the right deodorant, did not feed their children the right brand of cereal or their husbands tasty bread. Women were doomed to be seen as old spinsters for being smelly, gossiped about for having skinny, unhealthy children, or be divorced or cheated on by unsatisfied husbands. Sivulka says, "Such ads manipulated women's hidden desires to be sought after and well-liked and to join the successful middle class."[62] Assuredly, these ads depended for their power upon the depiction of normative femininity and sexuality, and on the alleged truth that all women wished to be "sought after." Women who were lesbians, who did not want to get married and/or have children, or who wanted a career were not shown at all. Like African Americans and other minorities, these "unnatural women" were not considered an audience upon which to focus.

Ironically, just as advertisers portrayed the independent woman to be a potential spinster, they soon recognized that with the winning of women's suffrage, this same woman was a powerful, potential consumer. Advertisers then linked products with the newfound social and political freedoms of women. For example, one advertisement in Marchand's *Advertising the American Dream* shows a glamorous woman with the caption underneath, "When lovely women vote." What happens when such women vote? The advertisement suggests they use Listerine toothpaste. Marchand states, "Consumption was the true realm for a modern woman's decision-making," not politics.[63] The truly modern woman could still keep an orderly and efficient house, play golf with "the girls," perform civic duties, and have the children bathed and combed when the husband came home from his tedious job in the city. This image of femininity was advertising's idea of the progressive, modern, American woman. Again, Marchand notes, "Advertising men, it appeared, were not only apostles of modernity; more significantly, they were *mediators* who counseled women on how to adapt without cost to a consumption-oriented modernity that was appropriate for feminine instincts and capabilities."[64]

Advertisers certainly understood themselves as "apostles of modernity" mediating to the consumer how to interact with the culture of consumer capitalism, and acted as such by envisioning their advertisements as "*secular* sermons, exhortations to seek fulfillment through the consumption of material goods and mundane services."[65] Despite the fact that they saw advertisements as "beginning to occupy the place in inspiration that religion did several hundred years ago"[66] they were not allowed to quote the Bible or use religious figures such as Mary or Jesus.[67] What they did use were "visual cliches as icons" that used the power of religious imagery to inspire the same kind of desire that religious icons or relics might evoke. Marchand outlines the icons used by advertising as (1) "Heroic Proportions";[68] (2) "Adoring Throngs";[69] (3) "In its Presence" (small group around a product, such as a refrigerator);[70] (4) "Holy Days, Poignant Moments";[71] and (5) "Radiant Beams" (nimbus or aureole effects).[72] For instance, for the iconic cliché of "In its Presence," Marchand describes an advertisement that depicts several elegantly clad women seated around a new Hoover vacuum cleaner.[73] As Marchand notes, the expression on their faces reflects a kind of divine ecstasy, or religious adoration. Even though the advertisements were not allowed to use explicit religious figures or blatant religious language, they sought ways to appropriate religious imagery. In this advertisement, there is no doubt that the image conjured to mind would be one of worship.

And one can imagine the quandary facing any artist to search for postures and facial expressions that would convey a true religious ecstasy, something far surpassing the exaltation these consumers showed in the presence of a refrigerator or vacuum cleaner. *Without directly competing with religion, advertising had appropriated the imagery of the sublime.*[74]

Another visual cliché was "Radiant Beams." Through this device, advertisements used lighting and relative position to give an almost "other-worldly" effect to the product. Often, the object became alive, a guest in the house to be served or entertained. The use of radiant beams was and still is a technique used to suggest the significance of the product. Advertisements would display the object alone, usually enlarged and towering ("Heroic Proportions" cliché used along with "Radiant Beams") over an adoring individual, or a group of people. And then, from an undisclosed source, one would see a beam of light lending luminosity to the object. It gave the product a heavenly glow, a sense of God-like approval. It seemed to suggest that if one invests in this product, one would find favor with God.[75] And not only favor with God, but with the product itself. By sacralizing the product through iconic visual imagery, it became a living totem, capable of making the consumer into its image, or fashioning itself into a household god. Thus, through advertising, and subsequently ownership, the totem and the individual were linked together, "vibrating sympathetically." Yet, it is not just the object that had imparted this quality, but the image created by advertising, and accepted by the collective that gave the commodity its true power.

Artwork and visual imagery were important for this period of American advertising because they taught Americans the new language of urbanity created by these visual clichés.[76] Even though copy was still being used, there was a gradual shift toward the visual as portraying the message for the advertiser. Through religious imagery in advertisements, consumers were beginning to adapt to "the modern icons of a faith in mass consumption" created by the "apostles of modernity."[77]

The apostles of modernity soon had to learn to mediate faith in a different kind of lifestyle. In October 1929, the U.S. stock market collapsed and with it many of the hopes and dreams of the good life that were being depicted through advertising. The fables of abundance soon became tales of scarcity, and advertising reflected such depressing times.

Because of the Depression, the use of artwork and visual images waned. Instead of using color and illustration, advertising turned to multiple typefaces and bold texts in order to grab the consumer's attention.[78] The *tableaux vivants* of the 1920s became too expensive to produce in the 1930s, so copy became expedient once again for advertising. As Sivulka notes, "The ads that appeared during the Depression even managed to look depressed compared to the lavish, colorful imaginative ads of previous decades. Agencies hired fewer prominent artists and set up in house art departments, many staffed by inexperienced, inexpensive commercial artists."[79] Two issues are important to note during this period. First, even though advertising did lose quite a bit of revenue during the Depression they did not stop producing images for consumption. What they did was to change their tactics in order to continue to get their message to the consumer. Scare and whisper copy became even more prevalent as advertisements were targeted at an individual's insecurities of guilt, fear, and shame in order to convince the consumer to buy.[80] Second, even though the country was in economic turmoil, Americans held on to the power to buy with a fervency that was not commensurate with the pervading ethos. Cross points out that ". . . many Americans associated status and even adulthood with goods. The Depression led to a frustrated consumerism more than a rejection of the capitalist system."[81] It was as if owning goods and luxury items were the signifier of the life once lived and the dream to be had once again after the Depression had passed.[82]

At the same time, consumers were beginning to question the legitimacy and truthfulness of the advertising industry. Even though individuals were creating their identity, in part, through the purchase of goods, there was a dawning recognition that advertisements were not always depicting the true nature of the product.[83] The answer to this public scrutiny was Consumers' Research founded in 1929 by Stuart Chase and F.J. Schlink.

Consumers' Research object was to make free enterprise work better by creating a better informed and more powerful consumer community.

Consumer education was supposed to raise shoppers from the ranks of the patronized and manipulated mass and to make spending a genuinely rational act, appropriate for a democratic community.[84]

Through Consumers' Research, the American public was represented by lobbyists who sought governmental control of the advertising industry. In the 1930s, a score of legislation was passed, the most important being in 1938 when the Federal Trade Commission stated "deceptive acts of commerce to be unlawful."[85] With this ruling, advertisers realized that in order to remain in favor with the consumer they needed to self-regulate and acquiesce to the wishes of the growing consumer movement.[86]

One of the most favorable inventions for advertising during this time period was the radio.[87] The radio became the guest in the home, the friend that made one forget all the troubles of the Depression. This was especially important for advertisers since the person who was home the most was the wife, and she, of course, was the primary consumer of the family. It did not take long for advertisers to realize what a veritable gold mine they had in the radio. Assuredly, advertisers were limited to selling the company name while not actually mentioning the product. Ad agencies produced the theatrical radio shows to which so many actors lent their services. Sivulka states, "In 1938, radio had surpassed magazines as a source of advertising revenue for the first time."[88] Eventually, print media would regain that place of primacy, but for a time radio reigned supreme.

The radio was not the only invention during the 1930s that would become a primary tool for advertising. The television was introduced at New York's World Fair in 1939, but unfortunately it had to wait for its entrance into American culture due to World War II. The War brought considerable changes to the U.S. consumer culture. As Sivulka notes, it increased industrialization, enabled mass production at "aircraft factories, shipyards, and ammunition plants," and mobilized the labor force to work for the War effort.[89] What became increasingly important was that individuals were encouraged to spend (and ration) so that others might have jobs. Many advertising agencies donated their artistic talents to the War effort (Rosie the Riveter posters are an example). Consuming became patriotic, and the War Advertising Council who launched the biggest advertising campaign in U.S. history made sure that individuals got the message.[90] Sivulka states, "Advertising manipulated powerful human emotions, frequently evoking fear and pushing patriotism as the war progressed. Explicit ad campaigns depicted soldiers dying or pointed out that they were 'over there for you.' "[91] What is important to note is that advertising, through its many incarnations since 1880, had now become entrenched as a part of U.S. culture through government sanction and related religious traditions. There are various reasons for this, but it cannot be overlooked that the War, and the government's use of the advertising industry to promote patriotism linked with religious ideals, helped solidify advertising's place in the lives of the American people.[92] For better or worse, advertising had become the primary mediator of the culture of consumer capitalism.

Yet, were Americans that easily manipulated by the lure of material goods and the promise of government security in a burgeoning Cold War era? Cross says, "Americans have a long history of tension between the pursuit of material pleasure and the quest for simplicity,"[93] and then asks incisively, "How in the first half of the century did Americans challenge and restrain this culture of consumption?"[94] The answer to that question is complex and reflects the multifarious nature of American society. Americans react and interact with the culture of consumer capitalism with an influential mixture of Puritanical guilt, the Protestant work ethic, strong individualism as fostered in a community, and capitalist greed and entitlement. Advertising works on all of these levels to appeal to the consumer. As has been mentioned above, advertising draws from culture and is also reflective of culture. It is only fair to say that since Americans have some of these traits by varying degrees, advertising will in turn reflect these aspects as it is expedient to their goal of creating a lifestyle and image for the product. Cross states, "In a country where personal freedom has been so closely identified with the right to buy and sell, it has been difficult to constrain consumption."[95] During the War, and after it, identity was created through the buying and owning of objects. For many, the ability to consume meant freedom, and, subsequently, became linked with what it meant to be an American.

1945–1960: "Realizing the American Dream"

After the War, Americans lived, once again, in a time of mythic abundance. The 1950s were truly a "flush time" as people began to consume more goods than ever before. This is made evident in that gross advertising expenditures between 1945 and 1960 quadrupled as new goods flooded the marketplace.[96] Many in the generation born after the War, known as the "Baby Boomers" had a lot of money to spend and manufacturers kept pace with this desire. Affordable single-family houses in new suburban areas gave many boomers new and exciting places to live and to house the latest gadgets, or "electric servants," such as refrigerators, freezers, and washing machines.[97] These new objects of technology soon became sacralized as a means through which boomers related to one another. In other words, it was not the possession of the freezer or the washing machine that signaled a new kind of middle-class living, but the image that owning such a product connoted. That image was one of technological advancement, sophistication, and leisure. Now, housewives did not have to waste the entire day on cleaning the house. With the new "electric servant" taking care of the chores, one's time could be spent more productively. Through image production, advertising changed a mere object of household drudgery into a commodity-totem imbued with the sacral power of consumerism.

Newness in products had to be visible and manufacturers planned object obsolescence in order to encourage more repetitive purchases. The material affluence of the 1950s meant that what had once been prewar luxuries were now considered practical household items, and manufacturers made sure that advertising reflected that required need.

> Postwar manufacturers recognized one promising characteristic of this new generation: it had more money to spend and was willing to spend it. This was a time when consumers could be persuaded that a lifestyle might be bought on credit, and they were encouraged to own two cars and several television sets and to shop excessively.[98]

No longer were visions of abundance and religious imagery considered efficacious, because as Fox notes, the consumer was being exposed to more advertising messages than ever before.[99] Advertisers persuaded the consumer to adopt the lifestyle of material affluence by saturating the crowded market with hard, fast-hitting images and short copy in order to catch the attention of the individual. Because of the saturation of images, Americans looked to advertising to mediate to them cultural clues. Due to the efforts of the War Council, advertising had become an entrenched part of American life, shaping culture and also reflecting, or mirroring parts of culture to the individual. In other words, advertising had become the great mediator by reflecting a type of ultimate concern for the culture of consumer capitalism. Fox quotes historian David Potter, in 1952:

> Advertising now compares with such long-standing institutions as the school and the church in the magnitude of its social influence. It dominates the media, it has vast power in the shaping of popular standards, and it is really one of the very limited group of institutions which exercise social control.[100]

One of the ways that advertising could implement such social control was through the great technological invention, the television. The television became a staple household item, a living entity glowing with its salvific blue light every night. Like the radio, it did not take long for advertisers to realize the power that television could have for their industry. Skeptical at first, advertising took to television once the FCC freeze regarding signal interference was lifted in 1952.[101] All of the shows were controlled by an agency that represented a sponsor, and many advertising agencies consistently argued and fought for the most lucrative shows. It was the confirmed rigging of quiz shows (as in the Charles Van Doren case) in order to get the largest audiences possible that gave networks final full control over television programs. By the 1960s, advertisers were running advertisements on several different shows and were considered by the networks to be "participating sponsors."[102]

Unfortunately for advertisers, commercials on television were regarded by the consumer as an intruder in the home. It was pleasant (and exciting!) to watch the pictures on the screen, but what most Americans found annoying were the commercial breaks that interrupted their favorite shows, or the constant repetition of the product's name during the show. To insure customer loyalty, advertising had to appeal once again to the power of the visual image and not necessarily to copy in order to assuage the disgruntled television viewer. In other words, just like the shows on television, the commercial breaks had to entertain. Advertising adapted and sold American culture through television while trying to maintain a level of decorous noninvasive behavior in order to stay current in the burgeoning technological consumer world. In other words, as a mediator, advertising had to learn new ways to remain culturally relevant, but at the same time not seem intrusive. Fox relates advertising agent Whit Hobbs's claim concerning the rise of technology and television: "The sky used to be the limit [for advertising's influence on American culture], but suddenly there *isn't* any limit. We can no longer conceive what the limit might be."[103] Advertising, recognizing a new market, not only presented sacramental objects of technology for consumption, but sold advancement through technology as an additional object for purchase.

Despite technological advances, there was a desire to return to seemingly traditional values of home, church, and strict moral codes of behavior.[104] Whether the return to these family values was produced by advertising and mirrored back to society, or vice versa, is hard to discern. What is important to note is that advertisers consistently reinforced the image of the white traditional family by depicting Dad as breadwinner, Mom as housewife, and subordinate and well-behaved ideal children in numerous spots using print and television. Despite the fact that women had been an effective and productive part of the economy during the War, women were expected to return to their normative roles as housewife and mother. These "natural" roles were reinforced through the images of advertising.

> . . . [s]ociety did not expect the woman to have a productive role in the economy. Instead, she was to find satisfaction in the narrow roles offered by conventional family life as homemaker, mother, and wife. Even as men continued to dominate the advertising industry, advertisements presented the woman's point of view as seen by men. Ads also constantly reminded the American woman of everything she ought to be.[105]

Even though most advertising showed women in the roles as housewife and mother, many women had actually been "Rosie the Riveter" and now had a taste of economic freedom. Such images of the

"Happy Homemaker" as the ultimate achievement for women began to be criticized by those in the reawakening feminist movement. Ironically, as Sivulka notes, despite the emphasis on the traditional family, at the same time sexually suggestive and permissive advertising began to make an appearance.[106] Women most certainly objected to their being depicted as sexual objects for the pleasure of the male gaze, but their voices went largely unheard.

The booming economy also created a smarter consumer and advertising paid the price for this educated shopper. Greater federal regulations were introduced after the fervor that Vance Packard's *The Hidden Persuaders* created in 1957. Packard's work was an exposé of the advertising industry's new selling tool, Motivation Research (MR), created by consumer researcher Ernest Dichter. MR was a methodology that used statistics and psychology to determine why people bought what they did. This analysis denied that people were rational beings capable of making informed choices, but instead, argued that individuals purchased goods that elevated their sense of security. MR argued that people wanted to feel good about what they purchased as a source of identity. Individuals did not simply consume goods because of the taste, quality, or look of the product, but they bought items because of how products made them feel. In his critique of MR, Packard argued that advertisers were shameless "hucksters" reminiscent of the carnivalesque discourse, bent on tapping into the psychological reasons that people would buy certain goods. He claimed that advertising used sex and security to make people want what they didn't really need, or create a desire they did not know they had. Commenting on MR, Cross states, "[H]e [Packard] lamented how Americans were taking their clues from the advertising and entertainment media rather than from themselves. The new affluence did not create a classless society. Instead, it produced a mass of insecure individuals each trying to define and display themselves through their goods."[107] And Stephen Fox adds, "Rather than starting with the products and proclaiming its virtues, MR began with the buyers and what they wanted, even if they did not know what that was."[108] It was not so much that advertising was actually subliminally manipulating the consumer with the new psychological approach, but that Americans did not like to think that their most precious commodity, namely freedom, was being exploited by some abstract entity aimed at convincing them to purchase various items.[109] This attitude was based on the rising fear of a nuclear war and the accompanying paranoia that was prevalent during the start of the Cold War. For many Americans, an ephemeral being that was supposedly duping them into buying unwanted objects resonated too sharply with the threat of an unwanted occupation by a hostile army. Actually, what MR tried to achieve was to create a group desire for a product, and thus convince the individual that by owning the object, he or she would now be a part of a community.

Assuredly, there was some subliminal aspects in advertising, but on the whole, advertising was straightforward, if unimaginative in its campaigns. Advertising, however, does not use subliminal messages anymore because it doesn't have to. The culture of consumer capitalism is so pervasive in current advertising that, as Durkheim's theories show, the consumer understands that participation in the consumer clan requires being obedient to dominant society by purchasing its totems. And how the consumer gains this knowledge is mediated through advertising's sacralization of commodity- totems. The suspicions of advertising, however, would become an established part of society's relationship with advertising. Fox states:

> In 1946, 41 percent of the American people found half or more of all advertisers misleading, and 54 percent said it played too much on the audience's emotions; in 1950, 80 percent complained that it led people to buy things they didn't need or could not afford, and 81 percent called for stricter government regulation; in 1952, 68 percent rejected testimonies as insincere.[110]

Advertising's golden era had certainly passed, as public sentiment toward the industry became distrustful and apathetic. And in response, the creativity of advertising in the 1950s seemed to reflect such boredom.

Fox claims that advertising during the 1950s was "safe and dull, without flair or distinction" and that a "creativity problem existed."[111] Unbeknownst to the industry, social upheaval and reform would propel the industry into a "creative revolution." What preceded this creative movement was the emergence of "lifestyle marketing." Sivulka describes this campaign as "the practice of segmenting the market based on the spending patterns of groups of consumers. Advertisers targeted specific income levels, consumer lifestyles, and interest groups, instead of directing their pitches at the broadest range of the buying public."[112] By studying certain demographics, marketers began to create lifestyle advertising in which they attached an image of affluence and style to the product. Similar to sacramentality, advertising's image production transformed an object into a symbol of prestige whereby individuals were linked with the image of the commodity-totems. A hierarchy of advertising images arose and the consumer noticed the difference. Once again, many aspired to be in the upper class, with the usual totems of wealth displayed for others to see. In this sense, the most famous ads of the time actually had very little copy, but were strong in representing certain images of style and distinction.

> The most striking ads of this period—the Marlboro man, the eye-patched patrician in the Hathaway shirt, the fortunate owner of a Polaroid camera, the woman who did (or did not) use Clairol—drew their power from a single, bold photographic image with little copy, sometimes no copy at all.[113]

These ads were not just powerful because of their photographic boldness, but because the advertisement had created a desired image or a personality that was linked to the product. As Fox says, "Customers were buying an image, not a sales pitch."[114] Individuals wanted to go to Marlboro country, meet the Hathaway man, and color their hair like the movie stars. In purchasing these totemic symbols, individuals became a part of the burgeoning affluent lifestyle, and reflected what may be rightly read as the ultimate concern of the culture of consumer capitalism.

The country was on the cusp of a social revolution, yet advertising lingered behind, refusing to see the increasing diversity and gender and racial frustration in the United States. Advertisers were still courting the traditional white American family, believing this to be their target audience, and often using gender and racial stereotypes to do so.

> From the standpoint of the advertiser, however, the prime market continued to be not city dwellers, but white suburbanites—the typical "average Americans" who also appeared in television, radio, and print advertisements. This well-off group read a lot of magazines and

watched a lot of television, from which many took cues on how they should live. In short, they were ideal targets for advertising. Yet all the white advertising excluded not only African Americans but residents of ethnic urban neighborhoods, the single, the widowed, and single parents.[115]

This exclusionary tactic would not last long as the Civil Rights Movement, which had begun in the 1950s, was now achieving cultural force as more African Americans and many women began to criticize the industry for images of racial and sexual stereotypes. In addition, the feminist movement was lending its voice to the need for change by demanding the end of sexual objectification in ads and equal pay for equal work. It was evident that advertising would have to change with the times in order to remain culturally relevant. Indeed, ethnic minorities and some women required that the commodity-totems represent a new image for their consumption clans. In other words, who got to participate as part of the dominant clan was shifting, and these new voices demanded to be represented as a valid part of the consumer society. In the next era, advertising would need to mediate these challenging desires by a new brand of copy and image-production.

1960–1980: The Creative Revolution

Social upheaval, turmoil, and reform were the defining characteristics of the 1960s and 1970s and advertising fought to keep pace with the times. In two decades, the United States experienced protestors marching on Washington demanding civil rights for African Americans, the assassinations of President John F. Kennedy, Malcolm X, Robert Kennedy, and Martin Luther King Jr., Neil Armstrong's landing on the moon, Americans going to war in Vietnam as students protested nationwide on university campuses, the Arab nations' oil embargo against the United States, which caused a huge oil crisis and recession, the renewed strength and vigor of the Women's Movement through a push for the Equal Rights Amendment, gays and lesbians demanding civil rights due to police brutality at Stonewall, and President Nixon's resignation after being caught in the Watergate scandal. The United

States was truly divided. As characteristic of any cultural institution, advertising cycled through these events, reflecting the pace of the country. But as much as advertising tried to develop with society, it did not maintain its previous level of influence. Advertising, which had prided itself as being the institution that created change and mediated certain standards, was now being reformed by culture.

> The reform waves sweeping down Madison Avenue, aside from the creative revolution itself, derived less from internal dynamics within the business, more from changes in society at large. Advertising— which sometimes claimed to foreshadow and direct social change— actually lagged behind the general course of events.[116]

Because of the Civil Rights and Feminist movements, advertising was forced to shift its tactics. Not only were ethnic minorities and women demanding equal rights under the law, they were insisting also on being represented fairly in the media. For many, advertising had always given cultural cues for the structure of family, religion, and education. But stereotypical depictions of women and African Americans were no longer considered acceptable. For a while, Aunt Jemima, the Cream of Wheat Chef, and Uncle Ben of Uncle Ben's rice disappeared (they are since back). African Americans, previously represented only as servants, cooks, or maids, were now shown in a variety of occupations. What became important was not just how African Americans were depicted in advertising but how they were being strategically left out of ads in order not to offend.[117] Madison Avenue began a campaign to market to African Americans by using celebrity endorsements of certain products and ceasing depiction of African Americans in demeaning roles. Unfortunately, although Madison Avenue was trying to reform itself they still did not keep pace with society. Sivulka relates, "Ethnic stereotypes died hard in the advertising industry. Advertisers continued to fantasize about a mythical middle America populated by white people and guided by traditional values. Yet such cultural homogeneity had never existed . . . [a]dvertisers typically avoided controversial and political issues and feared breaking the color line."[118] Old habits were hard to break, especially when most advertisers were traditional white males. Even though there was no true existence of a "cultural homogeneity," individuals were still grouped into varying consumption clans by advertisers' desire of a mythic white middle class. It is important to note that there was not just one clan, but many, and all were identified by the totems they chose to consume. Advertising does create an elite of clans, albeit chimerical, which is reflected in the ownership of certain commodity-totems that are expensive and impart class status. Through this class stratification there is an element of "pecuniary emulation," in that many individuals aspire to be a part of the fickle clan of privilege. In other words, the possession of wealth and its objects mirrors a type of sacramentality of ultimate concern for the culture of consumer capitalism.

The consumer of the 1960s was better educated and more inclined to individual expression. Advertisers sought ways to keep up with this new consumer, and did so by undergoing a creative revolution. Sivulka states that "the results were a new way of doing business, a revitalized creative approach, and an emerging social consciousness."[119] Advertising may have taken on a new social consciousness, but this was not necessarily because advertisers suddenly felt guilty for racism and sexism in their ads. In the end, Fox adds that "advertising cared more about sales than about education or social dialogue."[120] However, by being a new type of mediator through which women and minority voices could be visualized and heard, advertising won the appreciation and sometimes fought the admonishment of the rising counterculture.

The main aspects of the creative revolution were inspiration, creativity, intuition, and humor. The scientific approach to advertisements was replaced by a more folksy method in which the focus returned to the product.[121] But this focus was no longer so serious. One of the most famous ad campaigns was for the Volkswagen Beetle car created by the advertising agency of Doyle Dane Bernbach (DDB). In the heyday of big cars and long tailfins, how, the creators at DDB wondered would one sell such an unattractive car?[122] The ad showed the car, very small on the upper left-hand corner of the page and surrounded by wide open space. The copyhead said, "Think Small." Another advertisement for Volkswagen showed the car and under it the word "Lemon." By using self-effacement and humor, copywriter Julian Koenig and art director Helmut Krone launched one of the most successful and memorable ad campaigns in American advertising. Another ad was for Avis in which DDB broke the taboo for comparative advertising by saying, "Avis is only no. 2 in rent a cars. So why go with us? . . . We try harder." Hertz, although not mentioned, was first in the rent-a-car business. It was these kinds of self-referential ads that led the way in the creative revolution.

As the baby boomers got older and more settled, their children came of age and became rebellious. The age of counterculture, politics notwithstanding, filtered into all areas of life, from fashion to music to hairstyles. In addition, the individuals of the counterculture seemed to have a tenuous relationship with religion. In an age of free love, experimental drug use, and suspicion of governmental intrusion, young people seemed to be indifferent, if not hostile to their parent's traditional religions. This ambivalence toward religion signaled what has been called the "secularization of society." Advertising, through the creative revolution, sought ways to keep pace with this seemingly irreligious cultural trend by reflecting a lack of religious imagery in the advertisements.

As a result of the countercultural movement, individuals opted for style over opulent wealth as the rich attempted to blend in with the crowd in order to be "keen." As Cross states regarding economic status and class issues, "More important still, status was increasingly hidden as lifestyle. Distinction remained as significant as ever but increasingly took the form of 'individuality.'"[123] In other words, advertising had to adjust its commodity-totems to a new type of consumerism. The symbols that used to be powerful in representing and giving identity were no longer efficacious. To be rebellious was now cool, and advertisers worked to commodify this hip new way of living in America. Sivulka relates that "success was equated with originality. Understandably ads grew more outrageous to catch attention. The watchword became novelty. Innovation became an ideological commodity. Realistic art gave way to collages, psychedelic images, pop art blowups, and camp art parodies."[124] In other words, advertising commodified the counterculture and those who considered themselves to be a part of the movement. As Cross points out, "Counterculturalists became rebels through consumption: tie-dyed dresses *as opposed to* cashmere sweaters and pleated skirts, defined them. The 'counter' in the culture was very much within the confines of consumerism."[125]

One would not want to diminish the power of the counterculture by its co-optation into consumerism. The voice of the people fighting against racism, sexism, classism, heterosexism, and a corrupt government was, and remains, vital for any nation. But, as Durkheim has showed us through his theory of mechanical solidarity, a person is continually negotiating between individual and collective authority as he or she acts in society. One of the ways that advertising eliminated, or at least assuaged this tension was to co-opt the counter of the culture and commodify representations of it. Indeed, what is more important is the relative ease by which advertising was able to subsume so quickly the "rebellious" nature of a certain segment of society. Also, Cross adds that "such people still needed goods to communicate with others and to feel part of a group. Hip consumption was a substitute for new institutions, socially bonding rituals, and, of course, serious political action."[126] In a way, the counterculture may be understood as a period of "collective effervescence" as people came together to perform collective acts of rebellious consumption. The individual was still using totems to be a part of the group, but the totems had changed from being mainstream and the collective was now counterculture. In such a way, the counterculture was being appropriated by its opposite, and was being used to express a new understanding of ultimate concern in the culture of consumer capitalism.

Interestingly, although goods were used to link people together for a shared experience and relationship, advertisers also sought to target the individual as an expression of the rebellious times.[127] Advertisements related to the uniqueness of the person and at the same time subsumed the individual into the much-desired counterculture society. In this way, individuals felt a part of society but were not asked to compromise their sense of self. The manner in which this was achieved was advertising mediating to the individual "cool" products to consume.

At the same time, some women were raising their voices against advertising's continued depiction of women as submissive housewives, dutiful mothers, and sexual objects for the gaze of the male. It had been fifty years since women had agitated in a prolonged, organized manner for equal rights under the law, and the media were targeted as upholding the image that women were inferior to men by such organizations as the National Organization for Women and Gloria Steinem's *Ms.* magazine.[128] Many women no longer believed in the myth that one had to marry and have children in order to lead a fulfilled life. Some women delayed marriage in order to have careers, and rejected the notion that one had to be nice and well-behaved to be accepted as a "real woman." Issues of identity, as deconstructed through fashion and behavior in the 1920s, were once again reconsidered, as many women began to choose their own gender and sexual identity against what was considered to be the traditional, heteronormative relationship.[129] Unfortunately, advertising was quite slow to adapt to this sexual revolution and continued to depict women as subservient. Sivulka states, "But advertisers continued to address women in terms of 'idealized roles' rather than 'reality situations' because they had narrow ideas of what they thought reached women."[130] In other words, advertisers perpetuated sexist stereotypes because they thought that was what sold to women, but more importantly because they thought that was what their husbands desired.

Fox allows that advertising still showed women as "dependent on men" but he does note that from 1959 to 1971 sexist portrayals of women in ads did drop remarkably.[131] In response to sexism in advertising and in the general culture, Betty Friedan wrote *The Feminine Mystique* in which she describes the "problem that has no name." Essentially, Friedan explores the problem of depression in the educated, suburban, white middle-class housewife and her struggle with the expectation that women were supposed to find fulfillment in their roles as wives and mothers. Those individuals who did not understand the boredom of the housewife asked why, when her life had never been made easier with all the modern appliances and conveniences, was she so restless and displaced? Why did the nagging question of "Is this all?" keep arising as she went about her daily domestic chores?[132] Educated women, now full-time housewives were questioning their sense of identity in relationship to their husbands and children. In other words, white middle-class women were beginning to contest the idea of a dependent normative femininity that had been constructed through the culture and mirrored back to them in advertising.

With this rebellion, advertisers slowly changed some of their images. One of the most famous campaigns was the *Virginia Slims* cigarette ads in which the drudgery of housework for the dependent wife was juxtaposed to the newly liberated single woman. In this manner, women were freed through the discarding of old-fashioned gender roles and embraced smoking as new and modern. However, the power of this image was dependent on the knowledge of normative gender roles in order for one to understand the irony of the ad. So, even though the advertisement looked as if it was celebrating women's newly acquired liberative role, it was actually reinforcing what many knew to be the "norm" by reiterating the stereotypical role of woman as housewife.

The 1970s also saw the reprisal of the consumer movement of 1929 as laws were passed to ensure uniform safety and ingredient labeling in more products. Marketers achieved consumer confidence and individuals were allowed to express a sense of power in their economy.[133] Unfortunately, this newfound power would lead to a sense of helplessness as the economy went into a recession and a gas crisis. This was due, in part, to the Arab oil-producing nations (OPEC) enacting an embargo against the United States. As gas prices increased and lines grew, marketers feared the worse. Most Americans, however, did not conserve. Spending, it seems, was once again aligned with freedom and Americans were reticent to give up this patriotic duty. Cross states, "Just as in the 1930s Americans did not adapt to depression scarcity with an ethic of simplicity, so in the face of the 1970s energy crisis they rejected long-term conservationism. Consuming patterns that freely used energy were too closely associated with freedom itself."[134]

In this consumer attitude, we see how the culture of consumer capitalism had now become an "ultimate concern" in the United States. Spending, and how one should spend and on what goods, was most clearly mediated to the consumer through advertising. Despite the challenge from various parts of the culture to conserve and save, identity was linked too closely with the ability to spend. In the 1970s recession, many Americans did not care that oil was becoming limited; they wanted the freedom to continue to do what they saw as an American right, namely, consume.

Even so, advertising seemed to lose a lot of its influence as individuals became indifferent to it.[135] This, however, may be its most powerful tool, as Schudson has noted. Advertising had become so ubiquitous that, no matter how shocking or banal, it was now firmly entrenched as the mediator of the ultimate concern of the culture of consumer capitalism. How then to entertain or sell? Fortunately for advertising, as Americans moved into the 1980s, another boom period was looming on the horizon in the form of "Reaganomics," an economy that served the rich and ushered in new forms of decadence and wealth.

1980–2005: The Information Age: A Media Revolution

Many Americans growing up in the 1960s and 1970s thought the future would bring the Space Age as envisioned in such movies as Stanley Kubrick's *2001: A Space Odyssey* or George Lucas's *Star Wars*. Instead, the 1980s ushered in the Information Age and a media revolution that saturated the United States marketplace with the desire for personal computers. Apple introduced its computer at the 1984 Super Bowl by stating that "1984 won't be like 1984" in order to allay the fears of the consumer that computers might lead to a world like Orwell's "Big Brother."[136] And IBM used Charlie Chaplin's tramp to "put a human face on computers in order to get over computer fright."[137] Advertising, as in previous decades, was keenly aware of the role that technology played in the life of the consumer and sought to sell the new objects by building friendly, nonthreatening images around them.

As U.S. advertising became global and more entrenched as a worldwide institution, it shifted away from the hard-copy tactics of the lean recession years and once again began to "brand" cosmetics, cars, and clothing with images of opulent lifestyles. Sivulka claims, "Glamour, wealth, and style were back in vogue."[138] Indeed, this was the decade where the hedonistic maxim "Greed is good" was echoed by many Wall Street bankers as the United States saw the advent of the young, urban, professional, or "yuppie." This was a seemingly irreligious consumer who worked long and hard hours, often as an investment banker, made quite a bit of money, and wanted to spend all of it on the finest commodities. Shopping, no longer an activity just to purchase items, became a leisure pursuit in order to hoard goods.[139] It seems as if Veblen's conspicuous consumption had come full circle, although this time, there was a certain kind of desperate nature to this new consumer as he or she labored hard to showcase the newfound wealth and goods. More than any other previous period of advertising history, it is in this decade that we see objects imparting to the owner the sacramental image given to them by advertising, and thus adding a certain kind of value to the individual. As American society accepted the images given to them by advertising, it became even more of a mediator of ultimate concern for individuals.

In the following years manufacturers spent a great deal of money on image building for cosmetics, perfumes, and fashions. Style reigned over substance. Advertisers no longer described how their products worked; customers were left to fill in the reasons for the purchase based on their feelings about the product line, its image, and the attractiveness of the models showing it.[140]

Objects, with no inherent value to them, became precious and desirable, and so did the people that owned them. Image creation and thus branding has often been referred to as the new creative revolution of the 1980s.[141]

One of the images used in advertising during the 1980s was the return of sex (not that it was really ever gone) and symbolism. Because of the feminist movement and the strong presence of many women in the workforce, advertisers used ads depicting women as sexy and independent.[142] To be sure, almost all commodities became sexy, from jeans to perfume to beer. One memorable television commercial from the 1980s is the Enjoli perfume ad. In it, a business woman comes home to her waiting husband. In the ad she sings while stripping her business suit off, "I can bring home the bacon, fry it up in the pan. And never, never let you forget you're a man. 'Cause I'm a woman . . . Enjoli." In this ad there are mixed messages: She is the breadwinner for the home, yet she still is the cook. Not wanting to appear too threatening, she reminds the man that he is still the traditional head of the house by sexualizing her gender through strip-tease, wielding a frying pan, and, of course, spritzing herself with Enjoli perfume. Being a woman, the other part of the heteronormative binary, serves to constitute her husband's manhood. So, while the advertisement acknowledges this new class of working woman, it also reinstates, or rather reminds the consumer where she really should be: at home, sexualized by wearing Enjoli perfume.

Men's bodies also became commodified as sexual objects through Calvin Klein models and the mainstreaming of homoerotic impulses. Previously, this had been an untapped area for advertising. But with the rise of popular Hollywood "pretty boys" such as Tom Cruise and Brad Pitt, the male body became a site for advertising to construct male sexuality as a desirable object for both men and women. Since the role of women was shifting from dependence on men to one of freedom and self-reliance, men were forced to recreate and rejuvenate their image. As Andrew Wernick notes, "How ads have come to encode masculinity (and, correspondingly, femininity), then, partly reflects the way advertising has sought to secure men's identification, in sometimes unprecedented contexts with the standpoint of consumption itself."[143] In other words, using both homoeroticism and normative masculinity, advertising was now constructing men's bodies as sites for the objectifying gaze. For example, in an article in *Vogue* magazine called "The Brad and the Beautiful," Julie Baumgold asserts that men were now required to display their bodies as sites of beauty in order to compete in a culture that looked to the figure of an "ideal" body as a place for commodification. For support, Baumgold uses the theories of anthropologist Lionel Tiger:

> Once men could fairly well control their destiny through providing resources to women, but now that the female is obliged to create a living, he himself becomes a resource. He becomes his own product: Is he good-looking? Does he smell good? Before, when he had to provide for the female, he could have a potbelly. Now he has to appear attractive in the way the female had to be.[144]

Assuredly, Tiger's analysis maintains a heteronormative standard since not all men desire to be attractive to women, and vice versa. But it does show that new forms of male sexuality, along with female sexuality, were being regarded as a place where advertising could construct meaning.

Despite the use of sex in advertising and the conspicuous display of opulent wealth, rampant materialism, and greed, the 1980s and part of the 1990s were also characterized by a return to conservative government and strong, fundamentalist Christian values as exemplified in the presidency of Ronald Reagan and Republican Senator Newt Gingrich's *Contract with America*. This time, however, there was a new religious element to the rhetoric. Cross argues that what was implied by Reagan's "trickle down" economy, or "Reaganomics" was the "spending of the affluent was a reward for hard work" and the condition of the poor was such that they had "not learned market or family responsibility" and so were not privy to God's blessing.[145]

> These new conservatives [Reaganites and the Religious Right] saw the need to preserve family from the panderers of pleasure, yet they also encouraged materialism by denying the collective rights of consumers and tearing down the walls that held back the market from seeping into every corner of the American psyche and society. The result was a consumerism that moved even farther away from social cohesion and reality and toward an enveloping personal fantasy.[146]

In order to understand the fervor of the new conservatism, one should note the revival of and relationship between religious and political conservatism in America from 1980 to 1995, amidst what had become an increasingly multicultural and pluralistic society due to a massive influx of legal and illegal immigrants. Indeed, one may argue that the quest for a return to what the New Right had labeled as "traditional American family values" in which all of society based its ethical and economic structure on morals legislated by a so-called Christian government may have been a theocracy of reaction based on the American Jeremiad. As Sacvan Bercovitch has shown, the Jeremiad is one of the most enduring rituals of United States culture in that it tends to reinforce the conviction that Americans are a people set apart, chosen by God to demonstrate to the world a true merging of church and commonwealth, morals, economics, and politics.[147] Despite the neoconservative religious movement of the 1980s, advertising maintained its image of rampant materialism and individualism, thus reflecting the tone of neoconservative *politics* and the affluent aspect of the age. That is, even though politicians were attacking culture because of its lack of normative or traditional sexual morals, wealth as displayed through rugged individualism and oftentimes capitalist greed was rewarded as an appropriate reflection of American consumer morality. Advertising reflected the political agenda by the lavish images that were presented as symbols of an ultimate concern.

In the 1990s and beyond, advertising saw a waning of conspicuous affluence as the U.S. and foreign markets became more intertwined. The nature of consumption was becoming more globally connected as greater numbers of foreigners were consuming U.S. products and vice versa. Ironically, the global community of consumers had grown more fractured and diverse in its interaction with other markets and had created some difficulty for advertisers to know their audience.[148] No longer was there a uniform target consumer.[149] At the same time, consumers had become more cohesive under the rubric of American capitalism. In other words, due in large part to the Internet, people had less face-to-face communication with each other as they consumed, but were doing so as a global unit, demonstrating Western, and more specifically American values. What became evident for U.S. advertising was that marketing must become global also.[150]

Advertisers, realizing this necessity for a global marketing industry, have developed a strategy whereby two marketing tracks maximize saturation. One is a "global strategy" and the other is a "multinational marketing mix." Sivulka describes the two options: "The global strategy adopts a standardized marketing program with minimal modifications for different localities."[151] She goes on to add, "Most firms, however, found it necessary to customize their approach for each marketplace. With this multinational marketing strategy, each market is assumed to have different culture and competitive situations."[152] So, some advertisers will present an object using a homogenous image in print, on television, and the Internet in order to establish a loyal customer base.[153] This consumer will regard the object as dependable, and so will give repeat business to the company in return for the reliability of the product. For example, Coca-Cola's theme, "Always Coca-Cola," remains constant with its red disk and uniquely contoured bottle, but the scenarios used to employ this enduring icon changes. In this way, Coca–Cola mixes the two marketing options for maximum image saturation and cost-benefit returns.

One may go to Times Square in New York City in order to understand the saturation level of advertising since the 1990s. Every street, avenue, and building is covered with some type of advertising that glows with the insistent fervor of a culture that is reliant on selling products for its very survival. The gargantuan advertisements blink, flash, and stream across ticker boards, reminding any individual who walks through midtown Manhattan of what many consider to be the ultimate concern of American culture. It is so pervasive and enveloping one is unable to look anywhere in this town square without seeing an advertisement. Advertising is *literally* everywhere. As is often the case, one may find tourists stopped dead in their tracks on the sidewalk, using their digital cameras to record their New York holiday. But of what are they taking pictures?: The large Cup of Noodles display on 43rd Street. In other words, they are taking pictures of advertisements! In this sense, one may discern that Times Square is indeed a parody of itself, or more likely, consumerism. One may even find models walking around with minitelevisions embedded in their shirts displaying a two minute commercial, called "Adver-Wear." This concept consists of individuals wearing "T-shirts with 11-inch embedded video screens and four mini-speakers to make the wearer a high-tech walking commercial."[154] These advertisements were used by "Twentieth Century Fox . . . to promote its new Will Smith movie *I, Robot* in 10 markets. Fashion models wore 50 of the shirts—playing 2½-minute movie trailers on the flat mini-screens—in cities including New York, Los Angeles, Atlanta and Boston."[155] In this form of advertising, the body is literally inscripted with the totems of the culture of consumer capitalism. As Durkheim notes, individuals would often wear the symbol of their chosen totem on their bodies as markers that represented to others and themselves their participation in a particular clan. Certainly, individuals purchase commodity-totems that reflect their identity in a consumption clan, but in this example, the totems are purchasing the individual, by paying for the model, as a means to mark them as one of their own.

Interestingly, no one seems to notice, or be bothered by the frenetic, high-fevered pitch of the advertisements. It has become such an accepted part of U.S. culture, that if it was suddenly taken away, there would be a void. Assuredly, due to our fast-paced Internet world, this absence would probably be understood as an information glut, not necessarily a cultural vacuum. Because of its ubiquity then, advertising is not only a mediator figure, but also reflects the ultimate concern of the culture of consumer capitalism as it disseminated to the rest of the world.

> Worldwide markets have grown due to improved economic conditions and a desire for expansion. Advertising is no longer a Western phenomenon; it is now global. Countries like China and former Soviet Union once condemned advertising as a capitalist evil, but billboard images of Kentucky Fried Chicken in Beijing and McDonald's in Moscow have become the norm.[156]

Advertising may no longer be a Western phenomenon, but the values imparted through it are most certainly Western, or more likely American. Leiss argues that advertising is a privileged discourse because "the state of the economy is the predominant *concern* in public affairs" and "messages about goods surround us through our interactions with communications media."[157] In this manner, advertising mediates these American values by evoking the ultimate concern of the global community.

One of the ways that advertising mediates what may be rightly understood as ultimate concern is through certain shopping seasons as they are exported to Americans and the rest of the world. Note the Christmas holiday season. Every year on the day after Thanksgiving (now the day after Halloween), retail businesses open early, have special sales, hire extra labor, decorate their stores in holiday finery, and wait in anticipation for consumers to descend on their establishments. For a retailer, all of one's focus, training, and goals are channeled into this day and subsequent weeks when business outlets will hopefully show a profit. It has regularly been viewed as the busiest shopping day of the fiscal year for the last fifty years.[158]

In the *New York Times* on that Friday, the news coverage is quite scarce compared to the expensive full-page advertisements geared toward luring the individual to consume. This is indeed Debord's notion of "the society of the spectacle." He states, "The spectacle appears at once as society itself, as a part of society and as a means of unification."[159] That is, newspapers, as part of the media, participate in the culture of consumer capitalism by utilizing advertising to pay for their costs. Furthermore, they [newspapers] participate as sites of the culture of advertising, which conjoins the culture of consumer capitalism and the consumer who reads the text.[160] Furthermore, the television ads throughout Thanksgiving Day and afterward celebrate this spectacle of consumption by running hours of advertising. Even the local television stations have as their top story the shopping centers and malls. In an approving tone, consumers are told by newscasters that "The malls are packed with people buying gifts." For those who are sitting at home watching, is there a twinge of despair or guilt for not participating in this holiday ritual? Does one not feel a part of the clan if one is not purchasing the totems? Indeed, one's existence may be called into question if one abstains from the maxim: "I shop, therefore I am." Baudrillard argues concerning advertising:

> [B]ut the social function of advertising is to bring everyone under its sway. It is a moral code, for it is sanctioned by the group, and any infraction of it entails the apportionment of some measure of guilt . . . not believing in it still means believing sufficiently in other people's belief in it to adopt a sceptical stance. Even actions intended as resistance to it must be defined in terms of a society that conforms to it.[161]

The holiday shopping ritual is a collective act whereby advertising mediates the ultimate concern of the culture of consumer capitalism. Cross asserts, "Until recently, most intellectuals understood materialistic desire in consumerism as primitive, to be surmounted by a higher spiritual culture. They failed to see the ways in which materialism in the twentieth century had become more complex and how the physical and symbolic were intertwined in goods."[162] This intertwining of materialist desires with religion is something that is endemically American due to the form of capitalism that has taken root in the United States. This is not necessarily wrong in a moral sense. It becomes more complicated when there is a strict separation between the sacred and profane and materialist desires are linked to the profane. This separation is often purported by various cultural institutions, such as government and the church. But, as the history of advertising has demonstrated, even though these institutions maintain this dichotomy between the sacred and the profane, they are dependent on the culture of consumer capitalism and advertising, which ironically tends to blur this separation.

In this analysis of advertising, I am claiming that the desire for material objects is constructed as sacred as opposed to the traditional notion of materialism as profane. Indeed, the consumption of one's time with acquiring the material artifacts of capitalism may be considered vacuous, shallow, or even greedy. If anything may be asserted about modern or even postmodern advertising, it is that advertising depends on an understanding of the sacred and profane as diametrically opposed to each other, but does not necessarily respect the dichotomy as such. In other words, by destabilizing and intermingling the two categories, advertising reflects one of the strongest aspects of the culture of consumer capitalism: ubiquitous commodification. In fact, one may be so bold to assert that what is considered "profane" for advertising is to resist the life of consumption!

In order to achieve this form of ubiquitous commodification, advertising uses one of the most powerful forms of discourse in the past decade, brand identity. Brand identity is not necessarily a new form of advertising, since celebrities throughout the past have endorsed various products. One example is Bill Cosby representing Jell-O products beginning in the 1970s. But as athletes and movie stars have taken on cultural iconic status, their identification with various commodities lends a certain favored status to the product. Sivulka notes, "More than ever, however, brand identity has become one of the primary reasons that advertisers so closely link their products with sports; fans seem to identify as closely with the sponsor as with the sport itself."[163] Brand identity is possible due to the rapid growth of multinational corporations and their desire to no longer sell just a product but a brand. As previously mentioned, this is not necessarily new. Advertising has been trying to build brand loyalty since the 1900s. What is different is the pervasiveness of the brand due in part to corporate sponsorship. Most sporting events, jazz festivals, and rock concerts have advertisements posted all over the stage and its surrounding environs, and on the performer.

Brands are like the *churingas* mentioned in chapter 2, the bits of wood or stone that confer sacredness to the owner by the emblem marked on it. In this case though, the *churingas* are not removed from everyday activity, for they are reflective of the ultimate concern for the affairs of the clan. By changing the object into a symbol for consumption, advertising sacralizes the commodity-totem and gives identity to its owner. By wearing this mark, one is given status and power in the group.

Often, the public space and the body are branded with the identity of the corporation that is selling an object. In other words, they are marked with the emblem of the totem: "Wimbledon, brought to you by Adidas." And on many of the tennis players' clothing is the Adidas logo. By linking the product to the performer, advertising creates an image for the object. The implied statement is that wearing Adidas shoes will give you a cool image like many of the tennis stars. The desire for this image then creates a community, or clan of loyal consumers, who are linked together through the ownership of the branded product.

The product has been changed to a symbol with powerful repercussions for its owner. The object seemingly takes on a religious dimension of sacramentality. Just as the receiving of the elements of communion links a Christian community together, advertising, through its role as mediator, achieves clan cohesiveness through image creation and brand identity. In fact, *Adbusters* magazine quotes the advertising agency Young & Rubicam as declaring, "Brands are the new religion. The most powerful are the 'belief brands' like *Nike*, that spread a 'meaning and purpose to life' with the passion of the early Christians and Muslims."[164] And in an ironic twist of commodification, Jane Buckingham, president of Youth Intelligence, a company that seeks out new trendsetters, states that religion is also becoming a brand, thus marking its adherent as clan members:

> There is no question . . . religion is becoming the new brand. To a generation of young people eager to have something to belong to, wearing a "Jesus Saves" T-shirt, a skullcap or a cabala bracelet is a way of feeling both unique, a member of a specific culture or clan, and at the same time part of something much bigger.[165]

By transforming material objects (even religious objects) into symbols, consumers constitute a unique group through which they reiterate their identity through the ownership of their chosen commodity-totem.

> They [products] assumed "spiritual" roles, not in the ascetic sense of the Puritan, of course, but in the feelings of quasi-religious joy and contentment that came when consumers were accepted by others (and themselves) through their goods. In some ways, commodities became valued less for their utility (for they were seldom used up or fully consumed) than for meaning as markers of status, participation, identity, progress, or memory.[166]

Curiously, as Cross has noted, such participation does not require "self-denial," as understood in a religious sense, nor does it deny the "rights or existence of others."[167] He states that, in fact, the existence of the upper class as trendsetters and the lower class as imitators actually works as a system that includes the majority.[168] Advertising coincides with and reflects the social divisions of class, race, gender, and sexuality but all are eagerly welcomed to participate in the community of consumers as long as they are marked with the totemic emblem of their chosen clan.

One of the most impressionable groups of consumers who thrive on being accepted by their peers is young people. Advertising, through brand identity and corporate sponsorship, has managed to works its way into what seemed one of the least likely places for advertising to flourish, the classroom. This form of branding, known as Channel One, exposes school children to two minutes of advertising a day in between teenager style programming on a television set provided by K-lll Communications.[169] Schools do not actually receive any money for agreeing to do this, but they do get free use of the television and audio equipment for other activities.[170] In addition, many fast food chains, such as Taco Bell, Pizza Hut, and Subway have agreements with schools to use their products in the lunchroom. They are hoping that the kids will grow to like their food so much at lunchtime, that they will also convince their parents to buy their products for dinner. In other words, by marketing to children in schools, advertisers are hoping to create groups of young consumers who will remain loyal customers throughout their adult years. Again, in this way, advertising works to create a community by transforming objects into symbols through which individuals form a collective. Another way that advertising creates brand identity is by product placement in television shows and movies.[171] If one is watching television and notices one of the actors drinking a can of Coke during a scene, rest assured that Coca-Cola paid for that two-second advertisement. Marketers are hoping that by linking product usage to a favored TV star or Hollywood actor, the actor's fans will also want to purchase the object. For instance, on HBO's hit show *Sex and the City*, the main character Carrie often expressed her love for Jimmy Choo and Manolo Blahnik shoes. Because of the show's popularity, many young women went to various department stores to purchase these very expensive shoes or replicas of them. Advertising, through celebrity endorsement, had created a brand identity and a new community of consumers constituted through the ownership of strappy high-heeled sandals, a totem of normative femininity.

Another example of product placement is the futuristic movie *Minority Report* based on Philip K. Dick's novel by the same name.[172] In this movie, however, product placement is used ironically. Tom Cruise's character is running away from the authorities as he has been accused of a future murder. In order to escape detection, he must perform a gruesome act of self-mutilation and replace his eyes with someone else's eyes, as all citizens are now identified through a retinal scan. With his new eyes, he walks into a Gap store to purchase some clothing for a fellow fugitive. He is scanned and a hologram of a sales woman appears. She calls to him by name and inquires about the status of his last purchase. She then goes on to ask if he would like to buy some more items to coordinate with the past items. This example shows that although the Cruise character is known individually, and called by his albeit adopted name, his stolen eyes are also part of a larger data bank of consumers, which have literally been branded with the identity of the objects that their owner has consumed. He is subsumed into the group not just through his purchase of a pair of pants, but a "branded" pair of pants that constitutes his identity and makes him known in this futuristic society.

To be sure, Dick was certainly criticizing the rampant and tedious nature of advertising and the seemingly greedy nature of the culture of consumer capitalism. If the beginning events of the twenty-first century are any indication, there are many individuals who agree with him.[173] But Cross asserts that the Jeremiads of the anarchists, "downsizers" and "Adbusters," have failed because they have ignored the cultural power that goods have to convey meaning in an individual's life.[174]

> In the final analysis, the problem of the consumer culture was not that it threatened the cultivated individual. This essential assumption of the jeremiad from Veblen to Packard was wrong. Rather, the dilemma was that consumerism worked so well in meeting immediate needs that Americans found it difficult to want or even to conceive of ultimately more satisfying options.[175]

If advertising is merely an institution that disseminates information about goods to be purchased in the marketplace, then there would be no need for such Jeremiads. The problem concerning advertising is that it is not just a part of *laissez-faire* capitalism; it actually does shape and reflect American life and behavior. Very soon after the events of September 11, 2001, Americans were encouraged by President George W. Bush to show the terrorists that they had not "won" by going out and consuming. He stated, "Now, the American people have got to go about their business. We cannot let the terrorists achieve the objective of frightening our nation to the point where we don't—where we don't conduct business, where people don't shop."[176] In fact, echoing the ideology of the Religious Right of the 1980s and 1990s, when President George W. Bush compares the freedom of the United States to "terrorist tyranny," he almost invariably links freedom with some aspect of the culture of consumer capitalism. As in previous periods of war, like the soldier rescuing the flag for his country, buying products is how one expresses his or her patriotism. And how an individual knows what to purchase is mediated through advertising.

Sivulka declares, "A world without advertising would offer a far narrower range of goods, services, and entertainment—*and conceivably a nation without a clear idea of the American dream.*"[177] Just exactly what the American dream is and for whom is certainly a contested idea. To be sure, advertising works in a Durkheimian sense to coalesce groups of people into a community or clan through the ownership of certain commodity-totems. As Durkheim has argued, to worship a totem is really to worship the clan. By transforming objects through the rite of consumer sacrament into totemic emblems of affluence and status, advertising mediates to individuals the ability to become members of a globally branded clan that has as its ultimate concern the culture of consumer capitalism. To what extent this clan membership may be chimerical, or purport a sense of 'false consciousness' for identity formation, is an issue addressed in the remaining chapters.

Tracing the religious dimensions of advertising through this historical periodization has shown that advertising never existed in a social void. That is, there have been many cultural changes that have affected the way advertising has been received in American culture. Through this historical analysis, I have interrogated the form and nature of culture that has been articulated and expressed by advertising in the culture of consumer capitalism and how that has affected issues of identity for individuals. In this analysis, one sees that advertising and culture are mutually interdependent.

Because, or despite its cultural force, one of advertising's goals was to sell products. But it has never just functioned as a "salesperson." Advertising did sell objects, but more importantly, during the early twentieth century, it became an institution of cultural relevance by acting as a mediator of what may be rightly read as theologian Paul Tillich's ultimate concern. This relevance was achieved by showing the individual how to be a consumer. That is, individuals needed to learn about new objects as they were shuttled into the marketplace. Advertising, through the device of "brand loyalty" became a "teaching mediator" for the culture of consumer capitalism.

As stated above, the importance of tracing the religious dimensions of advertising throughout the history of consumerism was to show how advertising shifted in order to become and thus remain culturally relevant. One of the primary ways advertising has remained potent is through the use of religious dimensions to replace the traditional meaning providing institutions, such as family, work, art, and religion. Objects have been emptied of meaning through the process of production are given new meaning by the power of advertising. By using religious dimensions, advertising maintains a sense of the traditional institutions, but nuanced through the forces of consumerism. Yet, throughout this historical analysis, one might inquire as to why advertising has used, and continues to use, religion and religious imagery to maintain its cultural relevance. The answer to that question is the concern of chapter 4.

Chapter 4

The Religious Dimensions of Advertising in the Culture of Consumer Capitalism

A profound insight has been developed in modern literature namely, that one of the fundamental expressions of sin is to make the other person into an object, into a thing. This is perhaps the greatest temptation in an industrial society in which everybody is brought into the process of mechanical production and consumption, and even the spiritual life in all its forms is commercialized and subjected to the same process.

—Paul Tillich

The main assertion of this book is that though advertising is not a religion, it has religious dimensions that make it a culturally potent force. Up to now, cursory mention of three religious dimensions, in particular, divine mediator, sacramentality, and ultimate concern, has been made throughout the text. This hesitation was intentional in order to establish the position that Durkheim's totemic theories of religion were more illustrative of the function of advertising than Jhally's argument that it is a *fetish religion*. Indeed, in a manner similar to Durkheim's argument, my thesis may be accused of being functionalist, and rightly so; however, unlike Durkheim, it is by no means intended to be reductionist in the sense of a "descriptive reductionism,"[1] but more illustrative of what religious studies scholar Wayne Proudfoot calls "explanatory reductionism."[2] That is, the explanation offered may not "meet with the scholar's approval,"[3] but the "explanandum is set in a new context, whether that be one of covering laws and initial conditions, narrative structure, or some other explanatory model."[4] In other words, my argument is more concerned with the recovery of Durkheim's ideas as a hermeneutic for religious studies and advertising, and less with offering a prescription as to how advertising *must* be understood.

In this chapter, I want to show how the fetishism of commodities as it is implied in totemism is one of the primary ways that advertising acts as a divine mediator between the individual and the culture of consumer capitalism. Accordingly, what advertising actually does to an object by changing it into a product, and thus into a symbol for consumption and participation in the group is surprisingly comparable to sacramentality. Indeed, the transformation of the object into a product that marks an individual as part of a community that has as its ultimate concern the ideology of consumerism is a powerful illustration of the use of sacramental imagery in advertising. Recognition within and between clans is possible because the ultimate concern of advertising is to maintain the culture of consumer capitalism through individuals as they externalize their so-called propensity to acquire meaning-making objects and their desire to belong to society. Indeed, sacrament entails a mediator. There must be a presiding person or thing invested with the ultimate authority that blesses and dispenses the life-giving elements. Advertising, with the authority of the culture of consumer capitalism, accomplishes this task.

In current religious discourse, process theologian John Cobb, Jr., argues against the false consumption community as it is enabled in the culture of consumer capitalism for the sake of a more true community. Recognizing that individuals are constituted by the relationships they have with others, he states that individuals should be seen as "persons-in-community" rather than "individuals-in-markets."[5] For Cobb, the interdependence of humans can support a sustainable community that is a source of justice for the global economy. That is, the economy can support the community instead of the growth of consumerism.[6] Yet, the desire for individuals to constitute themselves in a group is exactly how advertising creates and sustains its power. People purchase goods that mark them as part of a consumption clan, since to be a consumer is to be a valid part of the U.S. economy.

Cobb believes that consumption exerts practices that destroy community and ecology.[7] What he desires is a radical change of the current economic worldview. Cobb states, "They [his points] require that Christians help envisage and implement a profoundly different economic order. Otherwise, the situation will continue much as in the past, when, almost regardless of avowed religious beliefs, economic practices led to the continued despoliation of the earth."[8] These practices are certainly evident, not only in the United States, but also in Second and Third World countries, as the American global economy exports its ideals and destroys other nations' infrastructures. Michael Schudson asserts:

> By our complicity, even if unwitting . . . we are contributing further to social injustice both in our own countries [sic] and in those parts of the world where poverty predominates. We act in league with the global corporations whose technology is "for enhancing private consumption," not for solving problems. We join Coca-Cola ("It's the Real Thing") and Pepsi whose influence in Mexico has resulted in "commerciogenic malnutrition" and we support the company campaigns which have succeeded in increasing the consumption of white bread, confections and soft drinks among the poorest peoples of the world.[9]

In the United States, however, what congeals a sense of identity for individuals is their recognition of each other in consumption clans through the purchase and display of the commodity-totems of global corporations. In the culture of consumer capitalism, individuals who are able to consume is "the real thing," or the seemingly ultimate concern of the U.S. economic worldview.

Tillich, speaking of "ultimate concern" asserts that, "A nation which looks upon itself as holy is correct in so far as everything can become a vehicle of man's ultimate concern, but the nation is incorrect in so far as it considers itself to be inherently holy."[10] Tillich was assuredly responding to the legacy of World War II when he posited the idea of a nation regarding itself as "inherently holy." Indeed, in chapter 3 we saw how nationalism when conflated with the culture of consumer capitalism supports his theory that, "The representations of man's [sic] ultimate concern—holy objects—tend to become his ultimate concern. They are transformed into idols. Holiness provokes idolatry."[11] In addition, Cobb states, "Despite the continuing strength of nationalism in the United States, the primary determinant of national policies is economic."[12] For instance, a relatively recent advertisement by Adbusters Media Foundation in the *New York Times* states, "Because my country has sold its soul to corporate power, Because consumerism has become our national religion, Because we've forgotten the true meaning of freedom, And because patriotism now means agreeing with the president, I pledge to do my duty . . . And take my country back."[13] This incisive "mock" advertisement seems to demonstrate that one should not discount the contribution religious ideas have for subtending the discourse of nationalism and economics in the United States. The advertisement also suggests that consumerism insinuates itself as a "false" religion.

Indeed, Tillich's idea that "all things have the power to become holy" provides one with the ability to ask several questions regarding advertising: What have become the "holy objects" in American consumerism? Does advertising as divine mediator accomplish this transformation? May we see advertising functioning in such a way that it is able to make all things have the power to become holy?[14]

Keeping these questions in mind, I want to demonstrate the three religious dimensions of advertising by employing critical theological studies to read the work of certain leading theologians of culture. Along with John Cobb, Jr., and Paul Tillich some other major scholars who construct theological critiques of the economy are M. Douglas Meeks, Sallie McFague and Mark Lewis Taylor.[15] Insofar as leading Christian theologians' theories are explored, it is with the hope of demonstrating the religious dimensions of advertising while critically engaging Christian symbols, since none of these scholars develop a specific account of the religious power of advertising.

Furthermore, comparison of McFague, Meeks, and Taylor's descriptions of the theological categories of mediator and sacrament, Cobb's analysis of ultimate concern, and Tillich's comments on mediator, sacrament, and ultimate concern will help illuminate the religious dimensions of advertising. The goal of theology, as feminist theologian Katherine Tanner has stated, is to "show an artisanlike inventiveness in the way [one] works on a variety of materials that do not dictate of themselves what [a theologian] should do with them."[16] All five theologians show their own "artisanlike inventiveness" in the manner in which they approach culture. It is my desire to engage not just their critique of culture, but their constructive theological insight in order to demonstrate the mediating power, the sacramental exchange, and the ultimate concern of advertising as it is expressed in totemic forms.

Advertising as Divine Mediator

The role of the divine mediator has been accorded a position of honor and prestige throughout religious history. John Macquarrie's work, *Mediators between Human and Divine* traces the place of the religious mediator as it is understood through the world's great religions.[17] In his text, he wishes to contribute to interfaith dialogue in recognizing the ongoing revelation of what he calls the "Holy Being."[18] Most mediators have acted as the mouthpiece of God, giving to their communities what they perceived as the divine directive for living a more holy and true life. The mediator in religion is thus a crucial aspect in understanding who or what the Divine is in relationship to human beings. Accordingly, this relationship will be important in analyzing advertising as a divine mediator in consumerism.

The great religious leaders, Siddhartha, Moses, and Muhammad of Buddhism, Judaism, and Islam respectively have generally not been regarded as divine beings. Christianity, however, regards its mediator, Jesus the Christ, as fully human and fully divine as codified in the Council of Chalcedon. This role of the mediator is unique in that the Holy Being desires to commune with individuals in order to have a closer, more intimate relationship with creation. As theologian Paul Tillich states concerning the issue of the mediator figure, "In . . . all of these men [Moses, David, Peter, and Paul] are mediums of historical revelation. And all of them, as well as the events themselves, point to something that transcends them infinitely, to the self-manifestation of that which concerns us ultimately."[19]

Let us examine Tillich's understanding of Jesus the Christ as a mediator in order to illumine the thesis that advertising acts as a totemic mediator between individuals and the culture of consumer capitalism. First, he states that the term often used for Jesus is that of mediator.[20] Second, what makes the role of Jesus as mediator ultimate for Tillich is the link between mediation and soteriology. Jesus is indeed a mediator but he is a *saving* mediator, one who bridges the gap between Creator and created, the Infinite and finite. Tillich states, "The savior does not save God from the necessity of condemning. Every mediating and saving activity comes from God. God is the subject, not the object, of mediation and salvation. He [*sic*] does not need to be reconciled to man [*sic*], but asks man to be reconciled to him."[21] In this passage, Tillich asserts that the mediator is not merely just a liaison, but a savior whose power and authority are derived from God. No activity takes place through the mediator except by God's blessing of such actions. It is God who has agency, who is the subject of mediation. And accordingly, humans are the object of this action. Even though Jesus as the Christ may be the mediator and savior, it is God who is uniting that which is estranged and that which needs to be reconciled.[22] Humans, and all creation, are the objects of God's divine love.

However, Tillich suggests that the concept of the "Mediator is not without theological difficulty."[23] He rejects the notion that Jesus as the mediator is a "third reality" upon which God and humans are dependent.[24] In other words, if Jesus is this third reality, then God "needs someone in order to make himself [*sic*] manifest, and—even more misleading—he needs someone in order to be reconciled."[25] For Tillich, God as the eternally reconciled does not need humanity for God's existence but God desires humanity to be reconciled to God.

Unlike Tillich's God who does not need humans for recognition, the culture of consumer capitalism is dependent upon advertising to reconcile itself to individuals. It achieves this reconciliation through advertising and humans redeem it by consuming the images of advertising. Advertising is the mediator through which the culture of consumer capitalism and humanity receive "revelation and reconciliation." That is, consumers are informed about products and their use through the images that are produced by advertising. The advertiser then creates the ad campaign for a product and also creates the image that is consumed by the individual. In this way, advertising mediates the message that consumerism desires to give to humanity. This act is revelation. How then are individuals reconciled? When a person purchases the product, and in turn the image/message that has been revealed in advertising, the two are brought together through the act of reconciliation between divinity and humanity. By the conjoining of subject and object through the act of consuming the advertisement and purchasing the product, consumerism and the individual are reconciled, until, of course, the object loses its salvific luster and the process is repeated with a new advertisement and object.[26] To be sure, this mediator role was especially apparent in the United States between 1880 and 1945. Advertising was instructive in that it showed the producer/individual how to be a consumer by describing new objects as they were introduced in the marketplace, and in this way acted as the "teaching mediator" between objects, humans, and the culture of consumer capitalism.

There is, however, a tenuous aspect in the theory of advertising as a divine mediator. Through Durkheim's theories of religion, we have learned that society produces its gods in an externalized form. Subsequently, the individual, existing in the collective, has created the culture of consumer capitalism as an ultimate concern, and so he or she is a very integral part of its production and maintenance. Tillich states concerning humanity's participation in industrial society, "Man [*sic*] is supposed to be master of his world and of himself. But actually he has become a part of the reality he has created, an object among objects, a thing among things, a cog within a universal machine to which he must adapt himself in order not to be smashed by it."[27] Thus, it is the collective that has created and now maintains advertising as its mediator for revelation and reconciliation through the culture of consumer capitalism.

For example, an advertisement may single out the individual, "You must buy these Jimmy Choo shoes!" but then will move the individual into a group for means of identification, "So that you (all) will be recognized as a part of the very hip 'Sex and the City' NYC crowd." The "you" of the example is the same grammatical form, yet it moves from the singular to the plural through the purchase of the image-laden commodity. In other words, advertising, through a system of totemic symbols unites people under the sign of the group through these transformed objects. But Durkheim's theories show that it is society which constructs and maintains advertising's role and accords it with this unifying power. In this paradigm, the dual aspect of creation and reception emanates from the same source, so that god and society seem to be the divine fountains from which all blessings flow.

How, then, does the individual learn to receive the "divine blessing?" Tillich understood the act of reception to have certain elements of divine action along with reciprocity when he argued that "mediation and reception are the same: the church is priest and prophet to itself."[28] Durkheim, foreshadowing Tillich in the sociological tradition, thought mediation and reception were similar because they are derived from the same source, namely society. The culture of consumer capitalism, then, takes on such force because it has become the externalized form of an internal regulatory god produced by the individual and recognized by the collective. The internal mediator becomes a coherent form in a culture that uses the externalized institution of advertising as its mediator. According to Durkheim, all of these aspects are produced by and given organization by the collective.[29] This coherence is given more power in that the divine mediator, namely advertising, is seen in the dimension of the religious. In this analysis, one would not want to assume as Tillich did that "The identity of reception and mediation excludes the possibility of the establishment of a hierarchical group that mediates while all the others merely receive."[30] As has been consistently reiterated, consumerism and advertising are dependent on gender, class, race, and sexuality stratification and oppression for their power. What is important is to recognize how individuals, even if they are alienated by the means of production in a capitalist society, work to produce and maintain some form of the culture of consumer capitalism through collective repetitive corporeal acts performed under constraint.[31]

Feminist theologian Sallie MacFague concurs with this understanding of consumer culpability when she states, "*All* of us are collaborators in this silence. It is not just 'big business'and timid politicians that do not publicly declaim what consumerism is doing . . . We *enjoy* the consumer lifestyle; in fact, most of us are addicted to it, and, like addicts, we cheerfully stay in denial."[32] In other words, advertising would not work unless someone was consuming the images that are produced by it. Advertisers rely on cultural recognition in order to mediate the message and sell the images connected with the product. To read it through a Durkheimian analysis, advertisers create the image and totems of the collective will so that individuals are constructed into consumers. But, is it as McFague queries, "the good life for all people and the planet?"[33] Even if one is to understand society as the place of production for advertising as a divine mediator, is it a sustainable construction? McFague allows that individuals are free to choose certain desires and wants, but how free are we when we are bombarded by 150 billion advertisements a year in the United States alone?[34] Assuredly, since 1960 to the present, advertising has become global through consumer capitalism and is the predominant economy in the world. McFague declares that we need to consider how we want to construct ourselves, as insatiable consumers or as individuals with the desire for a sustainable and just economy for all.[35]

Another way that advertising acts as a divine mediator for the culture of consumer capitalism is its ability to conflate needs with desires. In a similar argument to McFague's, systematic theologian M. Douglas Meeks interrogates the concept of unlimited growth as posited by modern economic theory in his text, *God the Economist: The Doctrine of God and Political Economy*.[36] Tracing the role of need in European capitalist history, he notes that it was not until Jeremy Bentham and John Stuart Mill recognized the shifting nature of the economy along with the rise of Britain's ruling class that the concept of need and the concept of desire became conflated. Through an ever expanding industrial capitalist economy, need was linked with what had once been considered aspects of desire, such as, insatiability, obsolescence, and the infinite.[37] This link was due in part to a new understanding of religion, namely a concept of God that was used by the ruling class and later appropriated by the U.S. economy.[38] Meeks states, "Whereas both capitalist and Marxist conceptions of needs based in nature steadfastly exclude God in formally defining needs, our economy nevertheless depends on God concepts to justify needs and patterns of consumption that are dehumanizing."[39] The role of needs shifted and became joined with desire, which had as its justification the ruling influence of the church. Indeed, reminiscent of the position of the New Right of the 1980s and early 1990s, Meeks accuses the church of participating in this development of consumption-oriented needs by asking, "Should not the church ask whether the public language of needs in our political economy has played a major role in shaping its worship of God, or whether its own understanding and worship of God plays a role in the way needs are officially defined in our society?"[40] The basic needs of food, clothing, and shelter later shifted to desires and then embodied what may be understood as Thorstein Veblen's "conspicuous consumption" by coding itself through the possession of expensive, gluttonous dining experiences, designer clothing associated with the ruling class or the cult of personality, and opulent homes in "nice" neighborhoods that were signs to others that one did indeed have wealth and favor with God.[41] How individuals understood these desire-laden needs was imparted to them in part by the power of advertising.

Meeks notes that another reason the concept of needs changed was because humans were portrayed as naturally insatiable.[42] Prior to this, an individual's need was recognized to wane as it was satisfied. As a response to the burgeoning industrial society, economists stated that all economic theory is based on the intermingling of natural bodily appetites with needs. Since it is natural to be thirsty, or become hungry, these aspects of nature were shifted into consumerism and thus the need for things also became part of the "natural order." In short, needs became desires for objects and were coded as "God-given." Meeks adds, "Any sense of salvation connected with repression and thus with economics has to be eliminated as irrational. Need satisfaction becomes simply a dimension of rational economic behavior."[43] And thus, the theory of "unlimited growth" was conceived.[44]

One of the most important aspects concerning the developing role of needs is its link to a traditional concept of God as "behind the market view of . . . pure decision."[45] This description of God is crucial because it is the authority from which advertising derives its power as a divine mediator. To recall, a mediator normally does not act on his or her own power but as he or she is given authority by the Divine. Advertising has received such a divine commissioning through the culture of consumer capitalism as it is justified by "Divine Infinity" and connected with human insatiability. Meeks argues that in a consumer society, God is seen as having an infinite capacity for choice; God is known as the Infinite as opposed to humans who are constructed as the finite. Meeks states that when one understands God as the Infinite who has the ability to choose freely with no limitations, and individuals as finite beings who have insatiable needs, the result is economic exploitative relationships: "The God who is sheer spirit and the corresponding human being who is sheer spirit support a society that focuses all of its economic problems on the spiraling increase in insatiable wants and the doctrine of growth which has become the secular religion of our society."[46] Furthermore, as Cobb states, "People who are content with their basic needs must be taught to have insatiable wants. Those who have prized spiritual values above material ones must be persuaded to put material goods first. When persuasion and indoctrination do not suffice, economic and political force must be used."[47] The infinite then is embodied in finite relationships of commodity exchange and necessitous expansion as it is mediated through advertising using the totems of the market. Meeks goes so far as to state that "human beings give themselves and their decisions over to 'the infinite' which is both symbolized and enfleshed in commodity relationships."[48]

As Durkheim's theories make evident, humans have created this consumer society of commodity relationships. Individuals construct and subsequently recognize the totems by which one purchases the infinite; indeed, the totems partake of the nature of the infinite through the totemic principle. Advertising mediates the knowledge of the totemic principle through image production and subsequent consumption of this image. The source of the totemic principle is the Divine, which in this system is really just the collective. Franz Hinkelammert eloquently summarizes the relationship between the finite and infinite commodity exchange as a

> [f]orm of social consciousness that corresponds to a situation in which human beings have delegated the decision-making power over their own life or death to a commodity mechanism for whose results they do not accept responsibility—*even though this mechanism is the work of their own hands*. This lack of responsibility is then projected onto a God who enjoys an infinitely legitimate arbitrary power, who is the God of private property . . . [49]

Individuals not only create this "commodity mechanism" through advertising but they also work to sustain it in collective rituals of commodity consumption, known in Durkheim's theories as "rituals of collective effervescence."[50] For instance, the front page of the *New York Times* on the day after Thanksgiving in 2004 has a picture of shoppers literally racing into a Wal-Mart in Geneva, NY, to take advantage of early bargains before the holiday shopping rush.[51] The headline reads, "In Annual *Rite*, Shoppers Mob Holiday Sales."[52] In the Business Day section of the *Times* on the same day, the front story is of three related women, and their *ritual* of consumption on the day after Thanksgiving, "18 Shopping Bags and 3 Empty Wallets."

We are then given a timeline and map of their shopping spree, including a list of the place, time, and amount of purchase. In addition to this annual ritual of consumption, note how one of the country's leading newspapers is acting as an advertisement of itself. For example, one shopper was reported to say in the article, "We bought the paper the day before, but there were so many ads in the paper and on TV, it was hard to make up our minds." In other words, the *New York Times* is being self-referential in that it is sustaining the culture of consumer capitalism by reporting on the collective rituals of consumerism by embodying advertising as story, or news. As Baudrillard states, "By means of advertising, as once upon a time by means of feasts, society puts itself on display and consumes its own image."[53] Advertising is an advertisement of itself, and thus of the culture of consumer capitalism!

The acts of shopping and consuming have become "religious" rituals in American culture, especially during the Holiday season, due to the mediator role of advertising. Meeks says, "Buying is valuable in itself. Once buying is seen as a way of dealing with guilt, failure, the loss of self-esteem, and the fear of death, it will be elevated to the status of worship."[54] In this system, everything becomes a commodity-totem, which allows the individual to participate in the consumption clan. The way that commodities become totems is through advertising as it mediates the Infinite through images that give "fulfillment and dignity" and let individuals know that "to want more is a sign that we are alive and more deserving than those with fewer needs."[55] That is to say, advertising mediates between the individual and the culture of consumer capitalism so that the person may become part of the consumption clan. One is "remade in the image and likeness of our own handiwork, we are revealed as commodities"[56] and in this revelation one is reconciled.

McFague and Meeks's arguments are helpful in deconstructing the cultural and theological problems associated with the culture of consumer capitalism, in that they argue for a theology that moves society from a regimented understanding of being merely consumers to citizens of the world who live "sustainably and justly with other human beings and life forms."[57] For McFague, this means a theology and an economy that are in harmony with a new understanding of the "good life." For example, McFague argues that by definition, globalization means "a radically interrelated and interdependent human population" that must be taken to the fullest extent.[58] Globalization and market capitalism must include an "economy of the planet" that does not sustain the concept of infinite growth. The planet is not able to uphold the consumer lifestyle that is so predominant in the United States and subtended by the institution of advertising. She reminds us that as a producer and a consumer one has an obligation as an individual and as one exists in the collective to live justly.

> We, the people, have the right and the duty to decide what the good life is for us and for our planet and then to ask the economists to devise ways of allocating scarce resources so as to bring about this good life. If economics is, as we have seen, about this allocation, then it is for society, not economics, to decide the context, the goals, within which that allocation takes place.[59]

Similar to McFague's redefinition of a more just globalization, Meeks argues for a Trinitarian understanding of the Holy Spirit by juxtaposing the predominant economic view of scarcity with a theological understanding of *pleroma*, or fullness.[60] Meeks views Christianity as a possible source of subversion by calling into question the deeply embedded notion of scarcity in the current economic worldview.[61] One will often see this "scarcity rhetoric" in advertisements: "Buy now while they last!; Only a few more weeks until this deal is closed!; This offer won't be around forever, so get 'em now or lose out!" These scare tactics are used to lure the consumer to purchase the product at that time by comingling the promise of instant gratification with the threat of scarcity. Yet Meeks wants to interrogate this coercive practice by suggesting a theology of *pleroma*, an acknowledgment of the fullness of God's blessings in the Holy Spirit and a life of spiritual abundance and justice.

> Nothing is deeper in the spirit of capitalism, and of socialism as well, than the belief that there is not enough to go around. The church, however, is called to live and organize itself out of the faith that God the Holy Spirit is willing and providing whatever is necessary for all persons and the whole creation to live.[62]

Meeks believes that scarcity should not be understood as lack. Assuredly, he recognizes that many people do not have enough food, water, shelter, clothing, healthcare, and jobs. Furthermore, our natural resources are being depleted by a selfish lifestyle of theoretically insatiable needs and desires. But as Meeks rightly points out, "Lack is not an illusion. Insufficiency is real enough. But insufficiencies, lacks, and shortages are not the same thing as the modern economic definition of scarcity"[63] that drives the culture of consumer capitalism. The supposed natural insatiability of humans is linked to the market's understanding of scarcity. The individual is blamed by the economic worldview for the current depleted condition of the world. But the source for one's insatiable character is coded as a part of the natural order, created by God, and upheld by traditional economic thinking so that individuals are relieved of any economic guilt. One may view this as a type of derivative insatiability. Scarcity, in other words, is understood to be a form of double predestination and therefore, God-ordained. In order to show that one is in the group that God has chosen, one consumes and owns products that have been blessed by the culture of consumer capitalism and mediated by advertising. One is then satisfied, for a time, because one is not participating in the culture of scarcity.

> In order to create a system of debt, on which our economy depends, we have to spiritualize both money and commodities. We have to convince people that if they do not possess certain products, they are not fully human. And thus a deep sense of scarcity is instilled in the minds and hearts of people through the media and their daily experiences. To want more is a sign that we are alive and more deserving than those with fewer needs.[64]

To put it another way, instead of recognizing that humans are responsible for the creation of this economic system of injustice, it is understood to be a part of the natural order that was given to humanity by God. Individuals then, instead of trying to work for justice and change, react apathetically to the oppressive effects of rampant consumerism since they have been led to believe by the modern economic worldview that such a system is part of the invisible hand of market forces and thus natural. But it is not natural. As Cobb states, "The economic order now dominating the world is . . . transforming the world into a primarily artificial place expressive of human purposes rather than its own."[65] And as McFague admonishes, one has a choice to select "which picture seems right, true, and good for ourselves, our fellow creatures, and our planet."[66] In addition, Meeks argues for a "shrewdness of faith" that calls into question the kind of unjust economics that are being perpetrated globally by the argument of scarcity.[67] He states, "The purpose of human life is not to consume or accumulate but to do justice. All needs should be defined in relation to that."[68] These needs are met, for Meeks, by God's own self-giving and righteousness as evidenced in the *oikonomia*, or economy of God. God is a "giver of bread," and a "doer of righteousness," which is most evident in the sacrament of the Eucharist.

The ritual of the Eucharist is a special moment in the time of the Christian community where the collective gathers together to share wine and bread in order to remember the justice of God in Jesus the Christ. As Meeks reminds us, "This distribution does not do away with every need, but it sees every need in relation to God's justice. This distribution does not do away with every hunger, but it transfigures every hunger and thirst into the hunger and thirst for God's righteousness."[69]

The Eucharist is an example of Durkheimian collective effervescence in that Christians gather together for a specific religious ritual in a heightened moment of spirituality, thus enabling them to live differently for a time. In order to continue to be efficacious, the ritual has to be rehearsed and reiterated at various moments in order for the community to remember that unique dispensation. Accordingly, and perhaps ironically, advertising also has its own collective rituals. By changing an object into a product and thus an image "of intimacy and happiness which we lack,"[70] advertising works by mediating the rituals of collective consumption by coding itself and objects as a type of sacrament.

Advertising as Sacramentality

In a recent advertisement, one sees two sets of beautiful diamond earrings. For the smaller set, the captions reads, "Thank you Bob," but for the larger pair, God gets blessed: "Thank you Lord." The small copy at the bottom of the advertisement states, "Nice in any size. Divine in a ½ carat or more. Make a bigger statement." The advertisement works on many levels, using beauty, piety, desire, shame, and humor. What do these diamonds represent? What makes them valuable? Is it their scarcity? Assuredly, they would not be precious if just one person thought as much; it is the collective's construction of diamonds as desirable that makes them so sought after. Since it is an accepted fact in the twenty-first century that diamonds are valuable, how are they maintained as such? How do consumers learn what objects are considered valuable by the culture of consumer capitalism? It was argued above that advertising as a divine mediator imparts such knowledge of products. One of the ways in which this relationship is maintained is through advertising having the religious dimension of sacramentality. In other words, objects become symbols of desire through advertising's bestowal of a type of divine grace that brings the community together for a time of recognition and remembrance.

As was demonstrated in chapter 1, Marx's fetishism of commodities shows how an object becomes valued in capitalism through its exchange value. It is this symbolic exchange that imparts value to the product, and also to the consumer, that is the key to understanding advertising as sacramentality. Subsequently, Durkheim's theories show how an object is given power by the collective agreeing on what functions as a totem for society. But, ironically, it is not the totem that is necessarily the most important aspect for the collective, but what the totem represents, or its totemic principle, that imparts the "sacred" to the society. As Durkheim states, "So the representations of the totem are more efficacious than the totem itself."[71] The totem bestows efficacy to those who adhere to the totemic principle. How the totem is transformed from object to image is a matter of sacramentality.

A sacrament is a religious ceremony or ritual that gives divine grace, or a symbol that communicates the sacred. Advertising as sacramentality is the means through which this grace is imparted to the individual when he or she purchases mere, shiny rocks that are coded as diamonds. By transforming an object to a product to symbol, the divine is present and subsequently imparted to the consumer.[72] Mark C. Taylor states, "[I]n today's world, money has become God in more than a trivial sense. Consumer capitalism generates a sacrificial economy, which eventually becomes all-consuming.

Through a process approaching *transubstantiation*, thing becomes image in a symbolic exchange that renders all reality virtual."[73]

In order to understand the transformative sacramental process in advertising, let us begin by examining the Christian understanding of sacrament, specifically as it relates to the Eucharist or Lord's Supper. The Eucharist is a ritual performed in the Christian tradition whereby the Last Supper of Jesus is enacted, commemorated, or symbolized, depending on one's Christian denomination and polity. On the night that Jesus was betrayed, while distributing bread, he commanded his disciples, "This is my body, which is given for you. Do this in remembrance of me." While giving them wine, he stated, "This is my blood of the covenant, which is poured out for many." Whenever Christians come together in a service of worship, they will often perform the Eucharist or Lord's Supper as part of the liturgy in order to reiterate their belief in the traditional understanding of the doctrine of substitutionary atonement. That is, Jesus, as God's only Son, was sent by God to live, and more importantly to die, for the forgiveness of sins; he is the reconciling mediator between God and humanity. Through His voluntary death and resurrection, He is the second Adam that restores creation to a pre-Fall existence of unity with the Divine.

There are three theories concerning the sacrament of the Lord's Supper. The first is the medieval doctrine of transubstantiation whereby the substance of the bread and wine are thought to physically change into the whole substance of the body and blood of Jesus. Only the accidents of the bread and wine remain. By reciting the liturgy over the host, the priest enables the conversion of the elements through God's blessing. The second theory is consubstantiation, associated with Martin Luther and constructed in opposition to the doctrine of transubstantiation. In consubstantiation, Luther proposed that the substances of the body and blood of Christ along with the bread and wine "co-exist in union with each other." So, the substance of the elements does not change but is considered a shared presence with Jesus' body and blood. The third understanding of the doctrine of the Eucharist is that of symbolism. That is, there is no aspect of change whatsoever, or even of a shared presence, but the Eucharist is a liturgical action that is used to commemorate Jesus' salvific actions of death and resurrection. The bread and the wine are merely symbols for enacting the rite as a remembrance of the Last Supper.

All three theories may contribute to our reading of advertising as sacramentality. But perhaps the best way to understand the sacramental aspect of advertising is a combination of the theories of consubstantiation and symbolism as they relate to Marx's fetishism of commodities. To recall, Marx states that an object is changed into a commodity for purchase in the marketplace due to the exchange value of the object. The exchange value of a product has to be interpreted and explained because meaning has been emptied due to the alienating forces of production. The fetishism of commodities theory states that as objects change from use-value to exchange value, the meaning and production of the object is lost. In other words, the object gets "mystified" or fetishized by capitalism. The value that is endemic to the process of human production and labor is given to and embodied in the object. This is where advertising appears. The meaning that has been lost in production is filled by the image-making process of advertising.

As I have argued in chapter 1, fetishism is an individualistic religion that is not centered in the collective whereas totemism is a group-oriented religion that uses objects as emblems for the respective clan. Since one of the most powerful aspects of advertising is that it works to move the alienated individual into a consumption clan by the power of suasive image production, advertising, then, may be better understood as having totemic dimensions that enfold the fetishism of commodities rather than acting as a *fetish religion*. This may be likened to what Thorstein Veblen called "invidious distinction."

> But it is only when taken in a sense far removed from its naïve meaning that consumption of goods can be said to afford the incentive from which accumulation invariably proceeds. The motive that lies at the root of ownership is emulation . . . The possession of wealth [and objects of status] confers honour; it is an invidious distinction.[74]

For example, like Jimmy Choo and Manolo Blahnik shoes, Prada bags are considered to be a desirable item to own. Indeed they are quite expensive, as their prices range from $1,590 for the Prada Python Frame Bag to $515 for the Flower Patch Body Bag. Both are advertised to reflect the lifestyle that would supposedly go with the ability to purchase such a bag. Let us call the people who are able to own such bags PradaClan 1 (PC1). However, in New York City, one may buy a Prada "knockoff" or imitation bag from various street vendors for a fraction of the cost, (between $10 and $20). Tourists and city dwellers flock to Canal Street to purchase their bags, either for themselves or as a present for a friend or loved one. Let us call the consumer on the street PradaClan 2 (PC2). In this PradaClan relationship there is an element of pecuniary emulation and invidious distinction because of the image that is associated with Prada bags through advertising. That is, PC2 cannot afford to buy real Prada bags like PC1 is able to, but PC2 wants to look and act as if he or she can. The power of advertising has generated such an image around a purse that people desire to be part of certain consumption clans (in this case PradaClan 1). Veblen states concerning the ownership of commodities, "It therefore becomes the conventional basis of esteem. Its possession in some amount becomes necessary in order to [have] any reputable standing in the community. It becomes indispensable to accumulate, to acquire property, in order to retain one's good name."[75]

It is not just the ownership of the commodity-totem and its subsequent consumption clan that marks it as having sacramentality. The object participates with the sacramental through the power and meaning that advertising has bestowed upon it. This sacred aspect is then imparted when the individual consumes the image that is attached to the object. Colleen McDannell states that the sacramental exists somewhere between "sacrament" and sign and symbol. Interestingly, "sacramentals also channel grace through gestures and objects but not to the same extent as sacraments."[76] The sacramentality of the object goes beyond it as merely a symbol; it is a *life-giving* commodity-totem that imparts grace. In the culture of consumer capitalism, the presence that is contained in the image created by advertising bestows itself as a symbol of grace to all who partake of the commodity-totem. But first, let us examine how Tillich describes sacrament to better illumine how, or even why, advertising uses the religious dimension of sacramentality in order to be a culturally potent force.

Tillich posits that Spiritual presence is a needed part of the sacrament in order for it to be efficacious. He believes that there is something primordial about the nature of objects and their ability to communicate "either by the silent presence of the object as object or by the vocal self-expression of a subject to a subject."[77] Tillich describes two "modes of communication" for the Spirit. One is the Word of God, the spoken elements of the liturgy, and second is the sacrament, the "objects which are vehicles of the Divine Spirit" and thus "become sacramental materials and elements in a sacramental act."[78] In his definition, Tillich not only allows for any ordinary object to acquire sacramental qualities but also for objects to impart a type of identity in the Christian community.[79] Objects are the signs by which individuals come to know and recognize each other.

But can the Christian community, (and I argue the consumption community also) experience a false sense of spiritual presence through sacramental objects? Tillich believes it can, in that "every sacrament is in danger of becoming demonic."[80] However, he does allow for a shifting nature of what objects get to be constituted as sacramental symbols for the Christian community. Tillich states, "For example, if a large number of the Spiritual Community's serious members are no longer grasped by certain sacramental acts, however old they are and however solemn their performance, it must be asked whether a sacrament has lost its sacramental power."[81]

Durkheim also states that a community's understanding of what is sacred changes as the culture develops. Through this change, one may see that what gets co-opted into the culture of consumer capitalism (as in the counterculture movement of the 1960s) depends on the will of the collective and its recognition of sacramental symbols. If an object no longer carries the same status as a symbol for "serious members" of the community, as in the wealthy, then that object will no longer be regarded as a valid totem for the consumption clan. For instance, as Prada bags become more easily duplicated and rendered inauthentic as signs of the upper class by the "knockoffs" of street vendors, advertising, with the aid of society, will pick a new object to transform into a symbol of wealth and prestige.

How then may we understand how advertising embodies sacramentality, and is related to Durkheim's understanding of totems as emblems of a clan? I argue that advertising takes a seemingly ordinary object and creates an image for it through an advertisement. As was demonstrated in chapter 3, how this is accomplished is based, in part, on the effects of historical and cultural production. Advertising then sells the product, but in reality it is selling the image attached to the product as it [advertising] draws from society certain aspects that are valorized. The product becomes an object, and one that is desired by the collective because of the mutually interdependent relationship of advertising and society. As it gathers strength through the ritual of collective consumption, it no longer remains an object but is transformed into a symbol. But, of what is this symbol representative? In a Durkheimian manner, it is society; that is, the collective is consuming itself since it has given advertising the mechanism (the culture of consumer capitalism) and the affirmation through which to create such a symbol.

In a similar manner, the collective ritual of the Lord's Supper brings together a community to celebrate symbols that remind them of who they are in relation to the Divine. Through the emblems of bread and wine, people are formed into a community of believers who recognize one another through the consumption of these symbols. It is not the mere elements, or objects that give them identity as a Christian clan, but the image which the bread and wine represents that points beyond the elements. Likewise, advertising uses sacramentality to group certain individuals into clans that have as their basis ritualized objects in totemic form. It is not the object one purchases, or more tellingly *does not purchase*, that gives identity in the clan, but the image the totem conveys to others that codes one's identity in the culture of consumer capitalism.

As argued above, this type of market sacramentality is one that is based on the stratification of gender, race, class, and sexuality. How does one resist such oppressive structures? As McFague has argued, we have a choice. By analyzing current economic theory, she attempts to construct what the sacrament of the Lord's Supper may look like in an "ecological economic model and worldview"[82] that stands against destructive consumption practices. Theologian of culture Mark Lewis Taylor also views the practices of advertising and consumerism as a source of oppression and argues for a "sacralization of material practice" by advocating an "emancipatory materialization."[83] Both of these theologians' analyses are helpful in pointing the way toward asserting a less consumption-based identity in the culture of consumer capitalism.

McFague uses the Parable of the Feast as found in the New Testament Scriptures (Matthew 22: 1–13 and Luke 4: 15–24) to critique the current economic worldview and its treatment of the poor. In her reading of the Feast, all are welcome; that is, "anyone is invited."[84] She notes that God's compassion for the lame, sick, and beggars of the world is, in the words of John Dominic Crossan, "more terrifying that anything we have imagined."[85] This "terror" exists because the individuals who are not allowed or discouraged from being a part of the consumption clan (the profane) are the ones who are sought after and welcomed. The supposedly sacred of the culture of consumer capitalism, the wealthy and the greedy, have refused the invitation.

McFague argues that in the ecological economic worldview, how we treat others and how the body becomes the locus is the way one may understand the culture.[86] We have seen that in advertising people are valued to the extent that they possess the objects of the culture of consumer capitalism. How one knows what objects are most desired is achieved through the symbolism enacted by advertising as divine mediator and sacramentality. Yet, what if the "sacramental symbols" were altered and changed? McFague seems to suggest that one would have a new view of the power of collective effervescence as made evident in the Eucharist that would then lead to a more economically viable and sustainable worldview.

> If one accepts this interpretation, the "table" becomes not primarily the priestly consecrated bread and wine of communion celebrating Jesus' death for the sins of the world, but rather the egalitarian meals of bread and fishes that one finds throughout Jesus' ministry. At these events, all are invited, with no authoritarian brokering, to share in the food, whether it be meager or sumptuous.[87]

She states that if one continues on in the current economic worldview and does not embrace this new Parable of the Feast, one should recognize one's participation for what it is: sin. Furthermore, institutions such as advertising that continue to perpetuate class stratification and theories of infinite growth based on a fictive understanding of human need as insatiable should be classified as evil.[88]

McFague uses decidedly theological terms to describe advertising and the culture of consumer capitalism. In this manner, she seems to want to view the current economic worldview as a type of "false religion." McFague's argument concerning the unsustainable economic worldview is a needed prophetic argument, insofar as Christian theology has often subtended the notion of the Divine by blessing the culture of consumer capitalism. However, my methodology resists using such strong theological categories of condemnation to analyze the role of advertising so that new areas of study may be discerned for religious studies.

Another prophetic voice is that of theologian Mark Lewis Taylor. Taylor posits a similar understanding of McFague's argument for "correct table manners" as a "sign of a just society."[89] In his essay, "Tracking Spirit: Theology as Cultural Critique in the Americas," Taylor states that "theology needs to participate in the spirit of critique at work in cultural practices."[90] Like McFague, he is working for a liberative praxis whereby emancipation through spirit is able to "break out" from oppression, and is also able to construct ways "where the negativities of domination are eradicated and mitigated in actions of reparation, restoration and connection."[91] One of the areas where he views this praxis as possible is in a new "christic valuation of material creation" [contra economic materialism] through "emancipatory materialization."[92] Taylor critiques the dominant economic worldview as classist, racist, and sexist, which is maintained by the structures of the culture of consumer capitalism and advertising. He also seeks to understand the earth's resources in such a manner that will value material creation, and subsequently distribute these resources in a way that reflects parity and symmetry. Taylor challenges the ideology of capitalist practices at its very core, including those practices that create and sustain the culture of consumer capitalism.[93]

One of the ways that Taylor constructs "emancipatory materialization" is through a prophetic challenge in understanding the sacramental practice of the Eucharist. He believes the sacrament loses some of its symbolic significance when the elements of bread and wine are "systematically abstracted" from their original substance; namely, the essential human needs of food and drink.[94] For Taylor, the Eucharist has become so ritualized that the original meaning of the offering matter has been lost.

Taylor states that Christian communities can enact emancipatory material practices by seeing the Eucharist in relation to individuals' true material needs, such as food, water, clothing, and shelter. "The Eucharist as sacramental practice, then, needs to become interpreted and structured as a practice that is central to an emancipatory resistance and recreation of human life in the face of classist distortions."[95] For this emancipatory practice to occur in the Christian community there will need to be a restructuring of the larger culture of consumer capitalism since, as Meeks argues, the concept of God is often used to uphold the current economic worldview.

Through Taylor's description of some current Eucharistic practices that seem to have forgotten "the original meaning of the offering matter," one sees aspects of advertising and its transformation of an object to a symbol whereby the means of production have also been lost. For instance, advertising has cultivated such an image with the Prada bag that one seems to forget that it is *just a purse.* As the Prada bag or the Blahnik or Choo shoes have become symbols of the sacramentality of advertising, the person who actually made the bag or shoes becomes incidental. The individual's need to consume, own, and display the symbol becomes paramount, and this is possible and desirable because the collective has recognized it as a suitable totem. How it was made, where and by whom are not considerations for individuals in consumption clans; the only concern is the ownership of the emblem as the marker of marked bodies. Consumption becomes a hoarding practice that reiterates the fictive insatiability and conflation of human needs with the fetishism of commodities.

In their theological analyses, McFague, Meeks, and Taylor offer a challenge to the Christian community's complicity in the culture of consumer capitalism. Through their normative critiques of the idolatries of consumerism, one may demonstrate the religious dimensions of sacramentality, but avoid a specifically theological analysis. However, by using religious discourse, one may have both the phenomenological or descriptive freedom of the anthropology of religion with the depth of a rich, theological discussion.

Advertising and Ultimate Concern

Paul Tillich, in his three-volume *Systematic Theology,* asks a profound, yet simple, question with regard to his concept of ultimate concern: "In what way does history influence our ultimate concern?"[96] Indeed, how does the ever-shifting culture of consumer capitalism influence what individuals believe to be the concern that is ultimate? As noted earlier in the introduction, Tillich defines ultimate concern as "that whatever concerns a man [*sic*] ultimately becomes god for him, and, conversely, it means that a man can be concerned ultimately only about that which is god for him."[97] To what extent then does advertising mediate "ultimate concern" to Americans? And what is the ultimate concern of the culture of consumer capitalism?

In this section, I argue that advertising mediates ultimate concern insofar as it participates in the culture of consumer capitalism. This participatory nature is evident in advertising's ability to create and sustain the culture of consumer capitalism by offering itself for consumption. Consumerism exists and flourishes by advertising mediating to the consumer what goods to purchase as commodity-totems. Yet, what makes ultimate concern a religious concept, if at all? In order to answer this question, let us examine how Tillich defines ultimate concern in his theological method.

Tillich argues that ultimate concern may be understood as a theological notion by arguing for its unconditional existence in relation to the great commandment found in Mark 12:29.[98] He states, "This, then, is the first formal criterion of theology: *The object of theology is what concerns us ultimately. Only those propositions are theological which deal with their object in so far as it can become a matter of ultimate concern.*"[99] Ultimate concern, then, is the foundation upon which all theology is based and is the only way to recognize what is the unconditional for the individual. The unconditional is found in all aspects of culture. Yet Tillich asks, "What *does* concern us unconditionally?"[100] He asserts that it is not an object, or even necessarily God,[101] but what gives the individual existence: "*Our ultimate concern is that which determines our being or not-being.*"[102] For him, what gives individuals ultimate concern is the "new being in Jesus as the Christ."[103] This "new being" is Tillich's theological norm, which is manifest in the church. Subsequently, the church is subject to the influence of the larger culture, and is able to be secularized by this culture.[104]

Since existence determines an individual's ultimate concern, one must recognize the relationship of nonexistence with finitude as part of the human condition. God then is the solution to the individual's problem about notbeing, and subsequently, his or her ultimate concern. Tillich states, "God is the answer to the question implied in man's [*sic*] finitude; he [*sic*] is the name for that which concerns man [*sic*] ultimately."[105]

Tillich suggests that there are other concepts other than God that can become ultimate concern for the individual. He refers to this substitutionary action as "demonic" and "idolatrous" as it is defined in relationship with the "holy." He states, "The holy is the *quality* of that which concerns man [*sic*] ultimately. Only that which is holy can give man ultimate concern, and only that which gives man ultimate concern has the quality of holiness."[106] One may ask, then, what is it in the culture of consumer capitalism that is being made holy and sacralized in order to convey ultimate concern? Tillich argues that the holy is made known to the individual by holy objects. Like Durkheim's totems that are not inherently sacred, neither are the holy objects in themselves holy. Objects point toward the divine. When they cease to do so and try to assert themselves as holy, then they become demonic. As these "holy objects" become the reflection of the ultimate concern for humanity, then they "are transformed into idols." For Tillich, justice is the corrective to such idolatrous behavior.[107]

In addition to idolatry, Tillich states that individuals are capable of recognizing a "wrong symbol of ultimate concern."[108] This capability is, in a sense, a "risk of faith," and part of what it means to be religious as humanity.[109] For in as much as individuals have faith, they show their capacity for ultimate concern. Tillich states, "The term 'ultimate concern' unites a subjective and an objective meaning: somebody is concerned about something he [*sic*] considers of concern. In this formal sense of faith as ultimate concern, every human being has faith."[110] In Tillich's assertion, we see a parallel to Durkheim's argument that "there are no religions that are false. All are true after their own fashion: All fulfill given conditions of human existence, though in different ways."[111] That is, for Durkheim, each religion points to some aspect of the Divine as it is discerned by the individual in the collective. No matter how odd the belief, or bizarre the rite, Durkheim believes the discernment of the religious points to some need for the individual.[112] For Tillich, this need is reflected in the capacity for faith, in that every individual is concerned about that which he or she considers ultimate.

Arguably for Tillich "the secular is the realm of preliminary concerns" because "it lacks ultimate concern."[113] However, Tillich does state that preliminary concerns are enfolded by ultimate concern.[114] Tillich notes similarly that the finite belongs to the realm of the secular. But conversely he states,

> The holy embraces itself and the secular, precisely as the
> divine embraces itself and the demonic. Everything secular is implic-
> itly related to the holy. It can become the bearer of the holy. The
> divine can become manifest in it. Nothing is essentially and
> inescapably secular . . . Everything secular is potentially sacred, open
> to consecration.[115]

Tillich makes a distinction, however, between the "secular" and the
"profane." For him, the secular is more neutral and does not have the
connotations of impurity that the profane does.[116] The secular has
the ability to become sacred, whereas as we have seen in Durkheim,
the profane does not. Tillich states, "We have seen that everything
secular can enter the realm of the holy and that the holy can be secularized."[117] Tillich's argument implies that varying secular objects or
practices have the capacity to become sacred, and divine aspects
also have the ability to become secular, or "lose their religious
character."[118] For Tillich then, there is a "unity of the holy and the
secular."[119]

Using Tillich's categories, it may be argued that the once secular
world of economic market activity has now become a "holy" center.
In other words, that which used to be the ultimate concern for many
people, namely God, has now been replaced by the culture of consumer capitalism. It is important to note that advertising does not
function *as* ultimate concern but participates *in* ultimate concern.
This is because advertising does not give the needed courage to face
the anxiety of nonbeing. Indeed, for an individual in a consumer
society, nonbeing would entail not consuming. Tillich argues that
institutions fail in functioning as ultimate concern because they are
unable to "supply the ultimate courage which conquers anxiety."[120]
In fact, far from conquering anxiety, advertising produces anxiety by
using tactics such as scare or whisper copy as illustrated in chapter 3.
For example, in a recent illustration in the *New Yorker* magazine, an
Iraqi man stands amidst his bombed out city wearing an "I Love
(Heart) U.S.A." t-shirt. Surrounding this rather shell-shocked looking person are thought bubbles such as, "Do I need a new car?"; "Is
my deodorant letting me down?"; "Are my teeth white enough?";
and "What's on TV?" This cartoon seems to state that liberation,
American style, *produces anxiety through the desire* to fit in as part of

the consumption clan. What kind of liberation is being perpetrated on the citizens of Iraq through global American consumerism? Worrying about body odor and buying a new car seems to be the legacy of freedom bestowed upon the Iraqi people. The current Bush administration seems to think that by liberating the Iraqi and Afghani people from dictatorial regimes, they will suddenly want an American kind of economy that coincides with this type of democracy. The ultimate concern of the United States is being exported through cultural insensitivity and imperial arrogance by assuming that the Iraqi and Afghani people will desire the American lifestyle of freedom through consumption.

Why, then, does advertising use religion? Tillich states, "Religion as ultimate concern is the meaning-giving substance of culture, and culture is the totality of forms in which the basic concern of religion expresses itself. In abbreviation: religion is the substance of culture, culture is the form of religion."[121] Advertising gives meaning to objects that have been emptied through the fetishism of commodities by filling them with religious dimensions. In this way, advertising, put simply, has become culturally powerful. Even if one is an atheist, there is still recognition that religion plays an important part in the shaping of all cultures, since, according to Tillich, religion and culture are interdependent.[122] For instance, in a special section in the *New Yorker*, an advertisement shows two people watching a sunrise (or a sunset) at "Inspiration Point." But it is not the sun at which they are gazing; it is an object for consumption. This advertisement humorously states that one doesn't go to watch the sunrise for enlightenment or spiritual rejuvenation, but looks instead at the luminescent elevation of one's favorite object as a source for illumination, in this case a symbol usually placed on the front grill of a car. The advertisement seems to be acknowledging that many Americans may not believe in God but they are "religious" in that they worship commodity-totems. Americans may not stop and admire the sunrise, but they do venerate the objects that they have created, namely consumer goods. Advertising, then, is not a religion, as Jhally asserts, or even a new kind of faith, but one does see its reliance on the faith and belief of society for its transformative power. Advertising, in this way, is the divine mediator of sacramental symbols that joins individuals with consumption clans who worship totems as reflections of ultimate concern.

If advertising uses the religious to be culturally powerful, may religion be used to deconstruct the ultimate concern of the culture of consumer capitalism? Process theologian John Cobb proposes an alternative to consumerism in understanding the "religion of growth" as an ultimate concern. Like Tillich's recognition that individuals worship "wrong symbols of ultimate concern," Cobb interrogates this religion of growth to determine if it truly is the "savior of humankind from destitution, drudgery, and misery."[123] Cobb notes that after World War II, the U.S. economy became global because it went unchallenged by the international community.[124] Cobb seems to suggest that what I have been calling the culture of consumer capitalism has become a global ultimate concern, or a type of "false religion," which he calls "economism."[125]

> If the world is to be dominated by a false religion, it is better to have it unified than divided into sects whose mutual enmity endangers all life on the earth. But if the religion is false, its monolithic character does not save us from the destructive consequences of its errors. This is how the situation appears to those of us who believe that economic growth is a false god, an idol.[126]

Perhaps one way to understand this "false religion of economism" is not to assert it as a purveyor of ultimate concern, but view consumerism as a "penultimate concern" that mimics "ultimate concern" by never really delivering the goods. Advertising may offer itself as a site through which the individual may construct a consumer identity; indeed, one is often "told" by advertising that this consumer identity is the identity that matters most. But it is in reality a chimerical identity that never gives ultimate satisfaction. As Mark Lewis Taylor suggests, "Maybe advertising steeps us in a frenetic, volatile penultimacy, reaching for, driving for, but being ultimately plunged into greater alienation . . . falling short of being able to live towards one's ultimate concern."[127] That is to say, individuals are never ultimately fulfilled by the ownership of commodity-totems, but are always left wanting more objects and images as a location for "false" identity construction through the insidious planned obsolescence of advertising.

For Cobb, the alternative to the "false religion of economism" is most clearly manifested in earthism that has an ideology, or religion of sustainability.[128] Cobb argues for a theological understanding of this economic worldview that points individuals toward worshiping the "true God," by being accountable to others and the environment in a "network of communities of communities of communities."[129] He states, "Earthism calls not merely for sustainable human communities but for human communities committed to the sustenance of the wider ecological communities of which they are a part."[130] The collective as an interdependent community, not the lone individual existing in the market, is where sustainable development takes place.

Cobb's vision of sustainable communities may be true of earthism as it is constructed against the culture of consumer capitalism. And yet, as noted above, an individual's position as part of a group is the strength upon which advertising relies. It is the need for an individual to belong to a community that advertising consistently co-opts. We have seen evidence of this mutual relationship in the history of advertising with its use of shaming tactics, and most recently, branding. For example, Nike has created a community of consumers through global advertising and product development. They even have their own city in Times Square: Niketown. Unfortunately, the corporation reaps its profits from cheap out-sourced female labor in the sweat shops of Indonesia, South Korea, and Taiwan.[131] This oppressive labor practice is a sign of the "false god" that Cobb wishes to expose, and is a form of what Tillich calls the "wrong symbol of ultimate concern."

Against this "false god," Cobb envisions a scenario in which individuals will "awaken from our disciplinary slumber" in order to enact change and live in sustainable communities that counteract the ideology of growth in consumerism.[132] Cobb believes if enough individuals recognize the limited capability of economism as an unsustainable worldview then "the very different religion of sustainability or earthism will appear as the evidently true one, and new economic thinking, ordered to sustainability will arise."[133] Cobb, however, does not think the religion of earthism, if it ever gets a chance, will put a complete end to the economic and environmental crises in which people find themselves struggling daily. He states, "It is a mistake today to look for ideal solutions. There are none. But it is not a mistake to look for ways to avoid catastrophes or at least to minimize those that may now already be inevitable and to prepare to rebuild in a sustainable way."[134] This confession, although admitting that there are no "ideal" answers, is a theological vision of hope. Cobb gives a coherent response to the "false god" of infinite growth, which is, I believe, an ideology subtended by the religious dimensions of advertising.

Cobb, McFague, Meeks, and Taylor all argue that the culture of consumer capitalism has become the ultimate concern of the current worldview. They are partly correct. The current economic worldview evokes ultimate concern as it is mediated by advertising, which creates collective rituals of consumption through sacramental commodity-totems. As Meeks states, the infinite and the finite are reconciled through the revelatory practices and rituals of consumption. My analysis, however, does not argue for a theological understanding of advertising, but for a more nuanced engagement with advertising's use of certain Christian symbols. Advertising has religious dimensions that are very powerful as cultural forces that work to systematically oppress individuals based on gender, race, class, and sexuality. These religious dimensions mediate a relationship whereby the individual is given identity in the collective through the sacrament of symbols that sustain a sense of ultimate concern. Yet, is this a "true" identity? Does advertising really give individuals a sense of identity-in-community, or is it better to understand advertising as creating false communities of people who are partly known by the objects they possess? Indeed, is there any way to resist ubiquitous commodification in the culture of consumer capitalism? Certainly, all of the abovementioned scholars are prophetic in their own theological traditions by advocating an "emancipatory materialization" as a way to resist Christianity's participation in the oppressive nature of the culture of consumer capitalism. With the help of their theological analyses, I have employed critical theological studies to engage the religious symbols of mediator, sacramentality, and ultimate concern as they are manifest in the religious dimensions of advertising. Having demonstrated these religious symbols, it is the focus of chapter 5 to construct a theory of identities that may help to "change reality" and disrupt the structures of domination wrought by advertising and the culture of consumer capitalism.

Chapter 5

Refusing to be an Advertisement: Enacting Disruptive Performative Identities against the Religious Dimensions of Advertising

Not only will I stare. I want my look to change reality. Even in the worst circumstances of domination, the ability to manipulate one's gaze in the face of structures of domination that would contain it, opens up the possibility of agency.

—bell hooks

When Thorstein Veblen wrote *The Theory of the Leisure Class* in 1899, he introduced the term "conspicuous consumption" into the general vocabulary and began a lively debate concerning the relationship of individuals and their ownership and display of objects. Since then, historians of culture such as Stephen Fox, William Leach, Jackson Lears, Roland Marchand, and R. Laurence Moore have provided the field of cultural history with richly detailed histories of advertising and consumerism. Some of these scholars have argued (most notably Leach and Lears) that as Americans moved into the twentieth century, the old agrarian way of life faded into urbanization. Cultural relativism, the erosion of the extended economic family, and the advent of a new leisure time began to permeate public and private life. As traditional institutions lost their influence, the need for meaning grew and advertisers developed ways in which their products could fill that desire.

As a result of this "urbanization," Americans are now living in the culture of consumer capitalism. Whether or not one subscribes to the ideology of capitalism, the fact that America's system of economics has become globally pervasive is obvious. How did society become so enraptured by image-making and consumption? One answer, suggested by Sut Jhally, and disputed by my argument, posits that advertising functions as a fetish religion whereby "the spirits of technology that invade the body of the commodity . . . supply the basis for a belief in its [advertising] power."[1] Another approach more complimentary to my thesis is that an individual's sense of self is constructed by and through the objects that he or she consumes. As Harvard economist Juliet Schor states, "The collection of brands we choose to assemble around us have become amongst the most direct expressions of our individuality . . ."[2] By purchasing objects as symbols of identity, the culture of consumer capitalism offers the means for identity-making; previously, this was a function of religion and other institutions.

As one may discern, the debate concerning the cultural role of advertising is lively, multifaceted, and far from settled. Cross asserts that commercialism (and thus advertising) won over other competing ideologies in the United States because "it *concretely* expressed the cardinal political ideals of the century—liberty and democracy—and with relatively little self-destructive behavior or personal humiliation,"[3] and also because "Americans found it difficult to want or even to conceive of ultimately more satisfying options."[4] In other words, social critics of advertising, or the "modern cultural Jeremiahs" as Cross calls them did not give a better alternative to consumerism. In fact, Cross believes that individuals "often choose consumption because 'real' community and 'true' individuality are difficult, frustrating, and thus boring."[5] To his credit, Cross does acknowledge that we need to understand why consumerism won so that we may "find ways of preventing it from absorbing human life."[6] These are all challenging statements, and ones I wish to try and answer in this chapter. As a "Jeremiah" of sorts, I have proposed Durkheim's theories of totemism as a hermeneutic for religious studies in order to posit that advertising constructs objects as totems as a means by which to group individuals into consumption clans. To be sure, I am not seeking to construct a "theological" theory of advertising; my main purpose is to demonstrate that advertising is not a religion but has religious dimensions. However, I don't want to leave the reader in the deconstructive phase, but I would like to offer an alternative view of consumerism by employing feminist theory as a means of resistance against the inscriptive nature of advertising. Often I hear from students the complaint that since we now have all of this information about advertising, how may we resist its influence? This chapter is an attempt to formulate a means of resistance against the often oppressive nature of advertising and its relationship to one's identity. By acknowledging the cultural function of advertising as that of having religious dimensions, I posit a "disruptive" religious and cultural critique of advertising by constructing a feminist counternarrative of embodiment.

But first, important questions still remain: how do advertising's specific religious dimensions of divine mediator, sacramentality, and ultimate concern shape identity? Conversely, how may a performative identity then deconstruct the negative impact that advertising has on the individual and the culture? Advertising creates subjects who then create meaning by reiteratively purchasing and consuming commodity-totems as a performance for a sense of self. I argue that identity in advertising is reiterated through a series of acts or performances, often, as feminist theorist Judith Butler insists, under constraint, which upholds the culture of consumer capitalism and seems to lend the appearance of substance. Through the repetition of such acts, identity constructs tend to take on power that gives them a reified objective existence. It is from this constructed, yet seemingly objectified existence that advertising abstracts in order to produce images that are desirable. But desirable for whom? There must be a way to rethink one's identity that is not dependent on advertising and its religious dimensions for subjectivity, (if one can call this kind of identity having any sense of Subjecthood). Indeed, as feminist theorist Judith Butler states, "But a critical genealogy [of gender] needs to be supplemented by a politics of performative gender acts, one which both redescribes existing gender identities and offers a prescriptive view about the kind of gender reality there ought to be."[7] By critically analyzing certain theological and religious categories, I have explored ways of thinking about the politics of cultural identity (more specifically, religious identity), and the religious dimensions of advertising, and want now to construct a different kind of identity that is not dependent on the consumption of advertising for its subjectivity.

Cultural Identity Formation

In postmodern society an individual's identity or identities are formed out of his or her everyday social practices in the culture of consumer capitalism.[8] In fact, John Storey states that cultural consumption is a *primary* way in which our identities are formed.

> Cultural consumption is perhaps one of the most significant ways we perform our sense of self. This does not mean that we are what we consume, that our cultural consumption practices determine our social being; but it does mean that what we consume provides us with a script with which we can stage and perform in a variety of ways the drama of who we are.[9]

For advertising, the everyday social practice of consuming goods is crucial in sustaining the culture of consumer capitalism. Drawing on my definition of religion outlined in chapter 1, advertising uses the religious dimensions of divine mediator, sacramentality, and ultimate concern to express itself as an immanent cultural institution that reflects the social. When an individual purchases a product, he or she is also buying a symbol that marks the person as part of a consumption clan. This participation and subsequent belonging gives identity, as was made evident with the example of the PradaClan in chapter 4. Yet, by giving identity to an individual through the collective, it also stratifies people into hierarchical clans that use their status as points of privilege, and subsequently, partake in oppressive practices. In other words, insofar as advertising bestows identity through the ownership of commodity-totems, it rewards those whose objects/images subtend normative practices of gender, race, class, and sexuality. Advertising, then, maintains the fictive practices of the normative binaries through sacramental symbols.

To be sure, it is not the object itself that imparts a sense of sacredness to the individual, but the image that is created through advertising (recall Durkheim's totemic principle), and which the person consumes for a sense of identity. For example, in a recent Mercedes-Benz advertisement, various photographs are displayed of the car and its owner. The caption at the bottom of the ad reads, "The most common photograph taken is with a loved one." There is the assurance that if one purchases a Mercedes-Benz, the luxury and prestige associated with such a car through advertising will be transferred to the consumer by the act of ownership. One will then become part of the MercedesClan. These individuals seem to treat their cars, and one would assume other objects, as cherished family members. In this advertisement we see that having one's identity connected to the image of a product, or totemic principle, is more efficacious than the product itself. This identity transformation entails a twofold cultural action: advertising, by mirroring certain aspects of society, must create the image for the product, and then the collective must accept and ritually consume the image as a form of blessing and reflective narcissism.

In order to understand advertising as a site for the production of identities, let us briefly sketch some of the history of research concerning identity formation and its relationship to consumerism. French Marxist philosopher Louis Althusser views advertising as part of an "ideological practice." This practice is the "transformation of an individual's lived relations to the social formation."[10] For instance, there are actual modes of being at the level of symbols and then there is the way one represents these symbols to oneself and the group.[11] In this context, advertising works as an "interpellation" (mediation). In an Althusserian manner, advertising "[c]reates subjects who in turn are subjected to its meanings and its patterns of cultural consumption. The consumer is interpellated to make meaning and ultimately to purchase and consume . . ."[12] In other words, objects that have been emptied of meaning in the production process are now filled with the meaning that advertising gives to them. Advertising mediates this new meaning, and through the consumption of both advertising and the object, the individual is constituted as a consumer.

Another theory of identity is an individual's participation in the collective rituals of the culture of consumer capitalism, or what Michel Maffesoli calls the theory of "postmodern tribes."[13] Drawing from Michel de Certeau, Maffesoli states that it is in the practice of everyday life that the postmodern tribes are made evident.[14]

The rituals of having a few drinks, sporting events, shopping, and holiday celebrations are all ways that "tribes" define themselves in terms of territory and existence. Maffesoli calls these gatherings, "rituals of belonging."[15] We have seen that advertising works through the postmodern tribes by the aforementioned brand identity and corporate sponsorship. Indeed, as mentioned in chapter 3, when the tribe gathers at a sporting event or musical festival, they are reminded of the power of advertising to "define territory and existence" by the ubiquitous advertisements that usually sponsor such an event. The commodity-totems of consumerism are linked to the performers, and thus the tribe (or clan, as I argue) discerns that it is a specific commodified object (including the performers) that links them together in a "performance" of consumer existence.

In other disciplines, such as economics, sociology, and anthropology, Juliet Schor and Douglas Holt outline several critiques that have been influential in the debate concerning advertising and identity.[16] The first is the "Economic Critique,"[17] associated with The Frankfurt School, and with the scholars John Kenneth Galbraith and Stuart Ewen. This critique, inspired by Marx's theory of alienation, argues that capitalist corporations require passive workers. These passive workers then become passive consumers. The result is a mass culture that is banal and entertaining rather than intellectually stimulating. Guy Debord calls this mass ideology "the society of the spectacle"; the more colloquial reference for this process is "the dumbing down of America."

Second, Schor and Holt note the "Cultural Critique,"[18] which appears in the work of Jean Baudrillard, (as well as Roland Barthes and Judith Williamson). How, Baudrillard asks, are needs and wants produced? His answer is that "individual desires are disguised expressions of social differences in a [mythological] system of cultural meanings that is produced through commodities."[19] In other words, Baudrillard believes that desires are produced by a code that people access through consumption.[20]

The third critique that Schor and Holt describe is "Consuming as Liberation."[21] According to this theory, consuming has become a democratic exercise in which the individual is free to reinvent himself or herself in order to become a constructive, creative person. Thus, consuming is not a passive act, but a liberatory one. Proponents of this critique are James Twitchell and John Fiske, who like anthropologists Mary Douglas and Grant McCracken, view material goods as the primary vehicle through which humans experience a sense of meaning.

Finally, there is the "Postmodern Market Critique," associated with Thomas Franks and Michael Schudson.[22] This theory states that everything has the ability to be commodified, from education, to health care, to personal identity. The premise behind this argument is that advertisers do not need to create meaning; they merely have to mobilize it. So a brand need not have a particular meaning, it just has to be attached to whatever or whoever has cultural value, such as iconic sports celebrities or Hollywood actors.

To be sure, all of these theories of identity formation are present in advertising to some degree. One theory is certainly not sufficient to describe how advertising works in order to persuade people to feel a level of devotion to their commodity-totems. What is important to remember is that identity is not necessarily created merely by consuming the object, but through participation with the image that is attached to the object through advertising. Durkheim's theories demonstrate how the feelings one has for an object are quickly transmuted onto the object and transformed into a symbol. It is the symbol that one loves and is grateful to, not the thing.[23] To recall, Durkheim uses the example of a soldier dying for his flag. The flag represents his country, but in reality is just a piece of fabric. Likewise, Tillich, echoing Durkheim, uses the image of a flag to argue for the participatory nature of symbol for the individual. He states, ". . . [t]he flag participates in the power of the king or the nation for which it stands and which it symbolizes."[24] Symbols not only point beyond themselves to the object they represent, but they also participate in the power and meaning of this represented object or idea.[25] In this manner, we may see advertising acting in a similar role, as that which references the culture of consumer capitalism, but is also dependent upon the culture for its power. By transforming objects into images, advertising creates ubiquitous symbols as a constant reminder that the culture of consumer capitalism is the institution that most deserves our love and adoration.

Durkheim's understanding of the individual acting to create sacred objects by putting himself or herself under the direction of the collective serves as an excellent lens through which to view advertising. For example, the collective inspires in its members the idea of religion. The collective then externalizes that feeling through projection and thus objectifies it as a part of reality. To achieve objectification, society fixates on a thing or idea, which eventually imparts sacredness to it. The sacredness of the object is not, as Durkheim adds, "predestined to it to the exclusion of others" but is, rather, part of historical circumstances that act together to produce this sacred object at this particular time and place. The thing is not intrinsically sacred; the properties of sacredness are added to it through the collective's imparting such qualities. Advertising functions in such a way by individuals being subsumed by society through the ritual of purchasing commodity-totems that impart status or power.

Surely, a capitalist economy relies on the promotion of individual self-interest, but it does so as the person is alienated from the means of production and then drawn back into a consumption group. There is always a fluid loop-like motion from individual to group on which advertising relies for its power. Simultaneously, part of the potency of advertising is that it constructs oppressive identities of gender, class, sexuality, and race through the consumption of commodity-totems. How then can one assume an identity that is liberatory and nonoppressive?

As we have seen, Peter Berger expresses a theory where externalized society becomes a world that cannot be wished away; once formed, it is outside the subjective claims of the individual, yet originates in the collective consciousness of human beings.[26] In this way, power is formulated and subsequently reified into practices of knowledge. Through this understanding of knowledge and power as it is perpetuated in advertising, one may analyze the construction of gender through other cultural binaries—black/white, rich/poor, and gay/straight—insofar as they also give identity. An identity located in these binaries is often maintained in order to reflect what is considered to be a part of the "natural order" mentioned previously in chapter 4.

If we may say this about cultural identity, then what are the implications for the assertion, or performative aspects, of a religious identity? Religion, understood in a Durkheimian manner, as an eminently social thing created by the collective and then imposed upon the individual through repetitive acts of collective effervescence, helps to solve this problem. That is to say, the only real substance of religion is that which is created by culture. As mentioned previously,

"In abbreviation: religion is the substance of culture, culture is the form of religion."[27] There is no stable identity or natural order for Christianity, Islam, Judaism, or Hinduism; instead, by having a performative religious identity, there can be a multiplicity of identities in each of these religions. As Mary McClintock Fulkerson asserts, "There are no given, natural entities, such as subjects, methods, or textual objects, once we recognize that these entities are constructed in discursive fields of difference."[28] And since there is no essential natural identity, then the prospect for fundamentalist division between religions and within a religion is lessened.

I have argued that advertising, through the religious dimensions of divine mediator, sacramentality, and ultimate concern, maintains the binaries of culture in such a manner that the fiction of a natural order is given legitimacy by appeal to the religious. I would like to offer a counternarrative, which may be understood as feminist theory sharing with McFague's "ecological economic worldview," Taylor's "emancipatory materialism," and Cobb's "ideology of sustainability" to expose how identities are indeed constructed and maintained in advertising. In order to understand this constructed narrative, one must look at the institutions that subtend the relationship of power and knowledge. For this analysis, Michel Foucault's theories of an embodied sexual subject as a location for power relations are helpful.

Policing the Body: Foucault's Theory of the Body as Inscriptive Surface

Michel Foucault states that the body is "acted upon, inscribed, peered into; information is abstracted from it, and disciplinary regimes are imposed upon it."[29] Yet, it is this form of materiality that enables the body to be a source of resilience against dominant modes of power. For Foucault, power, and its ability to inscribe discipline on bodies is crucially linked to knowledge.[30] He does not settle on an ontological status of knowledge, but considers it more a sociohistorical function of culture. Knowledge, then, is what culture agrees to be knowledge and what functions as such in society.[31]

Knowledge and power, then, are linked in a symbiotic relationship. For Foucault, knowledge is one of the major instruments of power;

what is considered true in society is regimented through practices of power and discipline on the body.[32] But whose body? As feminist philosopher Jana Sawicki notes, Foucault does not necessarily give a new theory about power and gender, but offers a different way to look at issues of identity that feminists have used to construct their own analyses.[33] In addition, Sandra Lee Bartky states that Foucault's analysis of power and gender relations is lacking because it does not interrogate the difference between male and female bodies. Bartky asserts, "But Foucault treats the body throughout as if it were one, as if the bodily experiences of men and women do not differ and as if men and women bore the same relationship to the characteristic institutions of modern life."[34] In this way, Bartky interrogates Foucault's essentialist assumptions concerning the body, or what seems to be presumed as the white, male body.

In advertising, one may see that power is indeed gendered in a patriarchal society. The female body, which must become a "docile body," willing to relinquish agency of sexuality and subjectivity, becomes a site of the dominant male gaze through various forms of media, including advertising. This gaze uses the relationship of power and knowledge to produce its patriarchal knowledge on the inscriptive surface, namely female bodies. For example, women's bodies, as seen on the front of fashion magazines such as "Cover Girls," are often flat, objective, "enfleshed" *surfaces* that reflect/mirror the male gaze.[35] Women's bodies re-present back to the onlooker, whether male or female, the politics of patriarchal power, which is then used to reinforce the ultimate concern of the culture of consumer capitalism. Indeed, I argue that in a patriarchal culture, women's bodies are often a symbol of sacramentality through which knowledge and power are reinforced.

Erving Goffman's *Gender Advertisements* is a key text for understanding women's bodies as an inscriptive tool for advertising and cultural knowledge. Goffman asks a disturbing and thought-provoking question in relation to advertising: "Why do most advertisements not look strange to us?"[36] He answers that advertising, especially of women's bodies, rarely portrays conditions that we have not constructed as part of dominant society. As Goffman affirms, advertising stylizes what is stylish, but most importantly, conventionalizes what is conventional, such as hierarchical gender roles. Advertising makes ideal what is stereotypical and vice versa. Advertising as a part of culture does not create situations *ex nihilo*, but abstracts from the constructs of reality. How one reads bodies, and who one defines as a "real woman," or a "real man" is based in part on how they are represented in advertising. This notion of hyper-domesticity was especially evident in the advertising of the 1930s and 1940s with the use of scare and whisper copy to shame individuals into performing their "correct" gender with the appropriate products. Like the intertwined relationship between knowledge and power, advertising abstracts from reality, and is also a location of constructed reality that mediates and defines social relationships.

This aspect of bodies as inscriptive surfaces and locations for advertising is more fully elaborated in Foucault's *Discipline and Punish*, wherein he gives a critique of modern society and the disciplinary practices used to regulate and control the body. Such practices are linked to the structure of the army, schools, hospitals, and prison, most notably in Jeremy Bentham's model prison, the Panopticon. This is a building that reinforces the manipulation of bodies and their surveillance. The Panopticon consists of a peripheral structure with a tower at the center. The tower has large windows that overlook the inner part of the courtyard. The edifice is divided into cells with two windows, one facing out and the other facing the tower. This is used to create an effect of backlighting so that the person in the tower can monitor all movement in the cell. Further, the person in the cell is always aware that he or she is being watched because of the effect of the lighting and the two windows. The person is also shut off from all communication with others, and is constantly visible from the tower. The effect of this constant gaze is "to induce in the inmate a state of conscious and permanent visibility that assures the automatic functioning of power."[37] As Bartky states, "[e]ach becomes to himself [*sic*] his own jailer."[38] Thus, not only does this discipline affect the body, but it is used to socialize the mind as well. The effect of this disciplinary structure is for the person to be brought into abeyance with the social order that the Panopticon represents. As Foucault states

The Panopticon, on the other hand, has a role of amplification; although it arranges power, although it is intended to make it more economic and more effective, it does so not for power itself, nor for the immediate salvation of a threatened society: *its aim is to strengthen the social forces*—to increase production, to develop the economy, spread education, raise the level of public morality; to increase and multiply.[39]

The male gaze functions as a Panoptical structure that works as an inscriptive modification of women's bodies into mere objects for the gaze. To be sure, "Cover Girls" function as flat, objective enfleshments of what is deemed appropriately feminine (and with its constructed opposition, masculine) by a patriarchal culture. Like Foucault's inmate, they are the "objects of information" for the male and for the male surveyor of women. For example, on the cover of a past *Cosmopolitan* magazine, former supermodel Cindy Crawford is wearing a string bikini. She has one hand tugging teasingly on the bottom string. Her lips are slightly open, as if in a dumbfounded, childlike manner. Thus, she is both sexualized and childlike, which represents two stereotypical forms of women's incarnation according to the male gaze, (or the women's fashion magazine, *Cosmopolitan*). For whom is the cover? Most of the readership, though not all, is female. In a compulsory heterosexual society, the cover seeks to allure the approval of the male gaze. Knowing that this gaze functions as the dominant form of approval and power in society, and that it is ever roving, women may be likened to the inmate in the Panopticon. A woman is always aware that she may be observed from the "tower" at any given time, so she takes over the job of surveying herself and modifying her behavior. She internalizes the gaze of the surveyor and the structure, which is patriarchy. "Cover Girls," then, are a tool in patriarchal culture that seeks to produce self-policing female objects that internalize the male gaze.

Another example is the cover of a *Marie Claire* magazine. The captions around the "Cover Girl" are "*Men* get naked and tell all," "Your best body ever," "The morning after—what *men* really think," and "*Men* who choose a wife from a catalog." It is odd that on the cover of a woman's fashion magazine there are so many captions about supposedly heterosexual men and their thoughts and desires, unless of course the magazine, its contents, and its readers are ultimately designed to incarnate the male gaze. And what the male gaze is incarnating is itself in the form of normative femininity and masculinity. Bartky states that women's bodies are increasingly becoming the sites of normative femininity in a presumed heterosexual society.[40]

But, even more interesting is the powerful ways in which advertising constructs a body for objectification. Bartky argues that a "panoptical male connoisseur resides within the consciousness of most women: They stand perpetually before his gaze and under his judgment."[41] Thus, the Panoptical power structure represented in advertising is a disciplinary practice used to regulate women as transformed symbols of sacramentality in order to reflect normative femininity. Bartky believes that the woman who buys a complete makeup regimen, invests in numerous hair products, pays for entrance to a fitness program, wears the latest fashions is akin to the inmate.[42] She is committed to self-surveillance under the watchful eye of patriarchy as the culture of consumer capitalism deems what the appropriate products are to buy in order to please normative heterosexual masculine standards. Indeed, the patriarchal culture, insofar as it is dominant, participates in the culture of consumer capitalism as a form of ultimate concern. Women's advertised bodies, as objects of sacramentality, become symbols of this ultimate concern.

Embodied Subjectivity and the Oppositional Gaze

Some women would not deny that female bodies are locations for the objectification of the male gaze. But the pertinent question is does the individual realize that he or she is susceptible to internalizing the gaze within one's self? That the surveyed and the surveyor exist within all individuals? When individuals look at advertising's representations of women's bodies, such as "Cover Girls," is there the awareness that one looks through the lens of the dominant other? Acknowledging this internalized sexism, let us look at three "oppositional gazes" that take seriously the "embodied and therefore sexually differentiated structure of the speaking subject."[43] These oppositional gazes will then serve as a foundation from which to construct an alternative or disruptive identity against the normative social constructs upon which the religious dimensions of advertising are dependent.

What does an "oppositional gaze" mean, or look like?[44] Let us concede that it is not merely a reversal, or replacement, of the gender of the person in the tower of the Panopticon. This would only reify the hierarchical objectification of human bodies, and be another incarnation for other types of gazes. The best way to deconstruct the male gaze is to dismantle the function of the Panopticon. This means that the mode of gazing at women's bodies (and all bodies) from dominant social locations, such as advertising, is destabilized. At this juncture, Luce Irigaray's "strategic mimesis," Rosi Braidotti's theory of "nomadic subjectivity," and bell hooks's "oppositional gaze" will be helpful in exposing the potent gender dynamic driving the gaze of advertising.

First, for Irigaray, mimesis is the act of claiming the position of the "feminine" in classical philosophical texts and unreading the phallogocentric discourse according to her own notion of the "feminine" instead of through "normative femininity."[45] Irigaray uses the image of a speculum, a curved mirror reflecting back on itself, instead of the flat Lacanian mirror that is used to reflect or mirror back the gaze of the person holding it.[46]

Interestingly, John Berger analyzes the mirror and its association with female embodiment and male inscription.

> The mirror was often used as a symbol of the vanity of woman. The moralizing, however, was mostly hypocritical. You painted a naked woman because you enjoyed looking at her, you put a mirror in her hand and you called the painting Vanity, thus morally condemning the woman whose nakedness you had depicted for your own pleasure. The real function of the mirror was otherwise. It was to make the woman connive in treating herself as, first and foremost, a sight.[47]

Thus women, determined culturally to be more vain than men, were given a mirror to indulge this inscription, and then blamed and mocked for being vain. Patriarchy has told women that they are more vain, and represented their bodies in such a manner as to perpetuate this "social fact." For example, Roland Marchand notes that advertising often used the image of a woman in front of a mirror or a vanity in order to construct what was considered essential "Woman."[48] In these types of advertisements, the mirror "served to epitomize women's supposedly unrivaled addiction to vanity"[49] and helped remind women that the "springtime of beauty" would soon fade if she did not hold on to it with the use of a proper beauty regimen.[50]

However, Irigaray offers the image of the speculum as a means to shatter the "male" mirror and allow women to hold onto a reflection that curves and reflects back to them their own identity and subjectivity, while enabling them to be a sight/site for themselves. Irigaray points out that in another time the speculum was a metaphor for depicting the truest picture of reality. She refers to the speculum mundi, the "mirror of the world," which was used to emphasize "not so much the reflection of the world in a mirror as the thought of the reality or objectivity of the world through a discourse."[51] By stressing the original meaning of speculum as discourse, Irigaray is deconstructing the Lacanian mirror and, one may argue, advertising as the mirror of society.

Second, Braidotti argues for a "nomadic movement of strategic mimesis" in the Deleuzian and Irigarian sense and for a "female embodied materialism."[52] Strategic mimesis for Braidotti is the act of replacing the standard, universal subject—white, middle-class, male, heterosexual—with one that is "structured by other variables, such as gender or sexual difference but also ethnicity or race,"[53] thus exposing the previous subject, or "universal" for its particular and specific approach.[54] "Being-a-woman" is the starting point for a new female materialism, which recognizes sexual difference as a sociological fact, and not necessarily an ontological statement of reality.[55] By qualifying the term "woman," one does not mold all women into the great universal "Woman" signifier, which subsumes multiple women's experiences into one homogenous being. One then has merely accomplished what one seeks to avoid: replacing the phallogocentric gaze in the tower with a different gender, and keeping the gaze still incarnated.

Last, bell hooks offers an insightful critique of the male gaze and how it is used to construct white womanhood as object and, consequently, dislocate black womanhood. By looking at cinema construction of black women's bodies she puts into practice "strategic mimesis and "female embodied materialism" by resisting the gaze and constructing one's own identity of subjectivity.

> . . .[t]he acts of analysis, of deconstruction and of reading "against the grain" offer an additional pleasure—the pleasure of resistance, of saying "no": not to "unsophisticated" enjoyment, by ourselves and others, of culturally dominant images, but to the structures of power

which ask us to consume them uncritically and in highly circumscribed ways.[56]

To consume uncritically, then, is to condone and be the surveyor within a female body. As Anne Friedberg states, "identification can only be made through recognition, and all recognition is itself an implicit confirmation of the ideology of the status quo."[57] hooks claims black women's spectatorship as a location for destabilizing white womanhood as object of the phallogocentric gaze, and relocates black women's sight as a location for resistance against the dualistic nature of mere surveyor and surveyed, or subject and object. That is, she exposes women's bodies as the object of the male gaze when she investigates the manner in which racism, and its use of black women's bodies, has functioned to create and sustain "white supremacist capitalist patriarchy" through advertising's stereotypical roles of "mammies," "hot bitches," or "castrating black matriarchs." This identity location invites black women to see themselves "not as a second-order mirror held up to reflect what already exists, but as that form of representation which is able to constitute us as new kinds of subjects, and thereby enable us to discover who we are."[58]

Disruptive Performative Identities

Acknowledging the theories of embodied materialism and an oppositional gaze, one sees that advertising depends on the stabilization and repetition of social performances in order for it to be meaningful and powerful in a Foucauldian way. I would like to argue for *disruptive performative identities* that destabilize and "contest the reified status" of the entrenched identity binaries—male/female, black/white, rich/poor, gay/straight—which the culture of consumer capitalism maintains through the religious dimensions of advertising.[59] In other words, we must consume *critically* rather than uncritically. Even if an advertisement seems to be gender, race, or class disruptive in its *performance*, such as the Virginia Slims "You've Come a Long Way, Baby!" cigarette ads, it is dependent upon the traditional notion of gender roles in order for the person to "get" the ad, or recognize what is being sold (and it's not just cigarettes). This reading of the Virginia Slims ad is an act of critical, disruptive consumption. Judith Butler asks, "In what ways is gender [and other binary systems] constructed through specific corporeal acts and what possibilities exist for the cultural transformation of gender through such acts?"[60] In other words, Butler believes that identity is "a *performative* accomplishment compelled by social sanction and taboo."[61] But what is the compelling social sanction of advertising? The answer is that an individual's identity is primarily as consumer, and the culture of consumer capitalism uses advertising to mediate ultimate concern between individuals and commodity-totems in order to reinforce this identity as a member of a consumption clan. And what is taboo for advertising? This would be to refuse to embody or participate in the appropriate consumption clan according to one's assigned place on the identity binary. Again, this is an act of critical consumption that resists being labeled as "hip" anticonsumerist counterculture and as a commodified location for dominant mainstream consumerism.

A disruptive performative identity means there is no preexisting identity, true or false, real or unreal by which to measure one's identity. For Butler, to posit a true identity would be to maintain a fiction of identity. In order to enact a disruptive performative identity against the religious dimensions of advertising one must resist the expressive nature that it desires. If one issues performative disruptive acts then advertising has no identity core upon which to reiterate and inscribe its sexist, racist, classist, and heterosexist models.

It is important to remember as Marx, Schor, and Williamson have argued that the culture of consumer capitalism is not natural. Yet, as Meeks and Cobb have noted, it attempts to code itself as the natural or the real through the use of religion and the ideology of infinite growth. The culture of consumer capitalism must be exposed as an entity that is created by society's participation and maintenance of it, just like the identity binaries are. Often these binaries are assumed to be essential categories of being, or a part of the natural order, but they must be exposed as fictive through disruptive performative acts, which are dramatic and tenuous so as to be nonreified and nonreferential.[62]

Through specular discourse and female embodied materialism, disruptive performative acts become a location from which to construct identities against the false community of consumerism. Women, and men, are able to reject dominant modes of representation found in advertising, and become subjects of their own identities. In other words, my theory works to destabilize advertising's objectified notion of bodies, and then seeks to construct an area of performative identities that valorizes *all* individual's experiences and aids in a formulation of a counternarrative of embodiment. By recognizing the constructed nature of identities one may attempt to expose the falsity of the natural order. Religion, as a production of culture,[63] must be included in the performative identities of the counternarrative. One does not give up identity then, but constructs a performative identity through a counternarrative of embodiment against the oppressive identities that advertising inscribes on the individual through its use of the insidious religious dimensions of divine mediator, sacramentality, and ultimate concern.

A Counternarrative of Embodiment

In conclusion, I have used a Durkheimian analysis to argue that advertising has religious dimensions but is not a fetish religion. As we have seen throughout the cultural history of advertising, individuals often construct their identity by engaging commodity-totems that are invested with the meaning produced by the discourse of advertising. How individuals know what objects to purchase is accomplished by advertising acting as a totemic mediator between the product and the individual. The image that is created by the advertisement and given to the object yields to a transformative process akin to sacramentality. That is, by changing the product to a symbol of invidious distinction, advertising imbues the object with an aura of the "sacred." It is no longer merely just a *thing*, but a commodity-totem that imparts a sacralized status to the individual as he or she is identified by a certain type of economic class. Through the ownership of such commodity-totems, individuals are thus formed into chimerical consumption clans, which in turn impart a fictive identity. Because the culture of consumer capitalism (as it is reflected in advertising) has become a globalized ultimate concern, this identity formation is crucial for the existence of an individual. By "branding" objects, and subsequently the loyalty of individuals, advertising empowers people to belong to, or mark themselves as part of this global commodity clan. But my counternarrative of embodiment seeks to give individuals the ability to enact a multiplicity of identities against the marking of bodies enacted by the religious dimensions of advertising through "embodied materialism," an "oppositional gaze," and "disruptive performative acts" that are oriented toward tolerance and justice. Judith Williamson reminds us, "But the objects used to differentiate us . . . the objects that create these 'totemic' groups are *not* natural, and not naturally different, although their differences are given a 'natural' status."[64]

This natural status was achieved in part through advertising reappropriating meaning from traditional institutions, namely religion, and imbuing objects with the meaning from these institutions in order to create product loyalty. These normative cultural locations were considered to be fixed, essentialized areas of identity-making for individuals. That is, previously, religion was an arena that gave people a sense of identity in a supposedly God-given natural order.

What I have argued is that the new industrial capitalism did not become a new religion; instead, it evoked religious dimensions as a way for the individual to make meaning in a quickly changing society. Beecher's testimonials concerning Pears soap as a means of imparting grace through cleanliness is a prime example of connecting a religious image to an object for purchase. When a consumer purchases a product, he or she is often buying the meaning that has been attached to the object through advertising, in this case, "cleanliness is next to godliness." And so, the identity that had once been constructed through religion was imparted onto a sacralized object through the image-making production of advertising. What I want to expose as fictive is that by evoking the discourse of religion, advertising relied on an understanding of identity as constituted through essentialist notions of gender, race, class, and sexuality. This reliance has been, and often is, oppressive to many individuals for their identity formation. And not only is it oppressive, but this relationship is tenuous at best because it relies on essentialized social binaries, such as normative femininity and masculinity, which do not embody the multifarious lived experiences of so many people.

Identity, then, is not based on a notion of the natural order, as constructed through advertising's reappropriation of meaning from traditional institutions, but rather on a social construction through which people are joined in nonreified "communities of communities of communities" as opposed to essentialized, chimerical consumption clans.[65] In this way, individuals may construct a counternarrative of embodiment that is not dependent for recognition on advertising and its religious dimensions.

Notes

Introduction

1. Sut Jhally, "Advertising as Religion: The Dialectic of Technology and Magic," in *Cultural Politics in Contemporary America*, ed. Ian Angus and Sut Jhally (New York: Routledge, 1989), 226. For his thesis, Jhally draws on Marx's metaphor, "the fetishism of commodities."
2. My work relates to the disciplines of theology, religious studies, and feminist theory and might best be described as "critical theological studies." This approach engages theological categories and discourse while maintaining a respectful distance from any profession of faith. That is, this methodology is analytical and descriptive of theological doctrines, but does not presuppose either faith in God or religious commitment. See Robert Cummings Neville, *Religion in Late Modernity* (Albany: State University of New York Press, 2002).
3. Jhally, "Advertising as Religion," 226.
4. Ibid., 227.
5. James Twitchell, *Lead Us Into Temptation: The Triumph of American Materialism* (New York: Columbia University Press, 1999), 57.
6. I have chosen William Leach's term "the culture of consumer capitalism" because it embodies several important areas of discourse. I trace the religious dimensions in the development of advertising in the United States. To be sure, one of the reasons advertising grew so rapidly was the burgeoning capitalist society of the early twentieth century. Although this culture may appear to be a coherent, unified economic system, its strength lies in its seemingly anonymous ubiquity, and also its classification as being distinctly American. One possible critique of Leach's term is that it tends to present consumerism as a homogenous entity without recognizing the movements of resistance within the culture of consumer capitalism. Although this may be a part of Leach's analysis, I most certainly do recognize countercultural movements as a part of the culture of consumer capitalism. In fact, my concluding chapter argues for such a "revolutionary"

movement by claiming disruptive performative identities against the oppressive structures subtended by advertising. I am grateful to Jesse Terry Todd for pointing out this problem of homogeneity in Leach's argument. William Leach, *Land of Desire: Merchants, Power, and the Rise of a New American Culture* (New York: Vintage Books, 1993), passim.

7. R. Laurence Moore, *Selling God: American Religion in the Marketplace of Culture* (New York and Oxford: Oxford University Press, 1994), 8, 9.

8. Emile Durkheim, *The Elementary Forms of Religious Life*, new translation by Karen E. Fields (New York: The Free Press, 1995), 9.

9. See Michael Schudson: "My subject is not advertisements but advertising: advertising as an institution that plays a role in the marketing of consumer goods, advertising as an industry that manufactures the cultural products called advertisements and commercials, and advertising as an omnipresent system of symbols, a pervasive and bald propaganda for consumer culture." See Michael Schudson, *Advertising, the Uneasy Persuasion* (New York: Basic Books, 1984), 5.

10. Although I consistently mention them throughout the text, chapter 4 is devoted to closely analyzing the three religious dimensions of advertising.

11. It is important to note that the next two religious dimensions function as illustrations of the religious dimension of divine mediator. However, this should not diminish their power. It is only by understanding the predominant role of advertising as a mediator that one can see advertising's capacity for other religious dimensions.

12. Paul Tillich, *Systematic Theology*, Volume 1 (Chicago: University of Chicago Press, 1951), 211.

13. Scholars who maintain this view are Ann Douglas, Sut Jhally, John Kavanaugh, Leo Spitzer, and James Twitchell.

14. See John Cobb, Jr.'s argument in chapter 4.

15. Schudson, *Advertising, the Uneasy Persuasion*, 12.

16. Ibid.

17. Mark Kline Taylor, *Beyond Explanation: Religious Dimensions in Cultural Anthropology* (Macon, GA.: Mercer University Press, 1986).

18. Ibid., vii.

19. Katherine Tanner, *Theories of Culture: A New Agenda for Theology* (Minneapolis: Fortress Press, 1997), x.

20. Ibid., 8.

21. Mark Lewis Taylor, e-mail correspondence, March 11, 2005.

22. Steven Lukes, *Emile Durkheim: His Life and Work: A Historical and Critical Study* (New York: Penguin Books), 34.

23. I do not intend to make a symmetrical correlation with Durkheim's theories and present society. Much of Durkheim's anthropological work

has been shown to be rather "arm-chair" and has subsequently been disproven. Rather, I want to invoke Paul Ricouer's analysis when he states that "metaphor is the rhetorical process by which discourse unleashes the power that certain fictions have to redescribe reality." What I seek to do is discover how Durkheim's theories of religion may be useful as an interpretive key in "redescribing" certain present religious discourse and it relationship with advertising. Paul Ricouer, *The Rule of Metaphor* (Toronto: University of Toronto Press, 1977), 7.

Chapter 1 Totemic Desires

Portions of this chapter were first published as a supplementary article, "Advertising" by Tricia Sheffield in *Religion and American Cultures: An Encyclopedia of Traditions, Diversity, and Popular Expressions*, Volume 2, edited by Gary Laderman and Luis Leon (Santa Barbara, CA: ABC-CLIO, 2003), 445–446. Specifically, see pages 18–19.

1. In chapter 2, the contributions of E.B. Tylor, George Frazer, and Emile Durkheim are discussed.
2. See Daniel Pals, *Seven Theories of Religion* (New York: Oxford University Press, 1996). I have chosen these four theorists because they are all in the tradition of Durkheim and help illuminate Durkheim's theories of religion.
3. Durkheim's theories of religion are functionalist and thus have been accused of having reductionist conclusions.
4. Pals, *Seven Theories of Religion*, 66.
5. Ibid., 133.
6. Ibid., 138.
7. Ibid., 143.
8. Ibid., 235.
9. Ibid., 239.
10. Clifford Geertz, "Religion as a Cultural System," in *Interpretation of Cultures*, 89 as quoted in Pals, *Seven Theories of Religion*, 244.
11. Pals, *Seven Theories of Religion*, 261.
12. Sarah Beckwith, *Christ's Body: Identity, Culture and Society in Late Medieval Writings* (London and New York: Routledge, 1993), 7.
13. Grace M. Jantzen, *Power, Gender and Christian Mysticism* (Cambridge: Cambridge University Press, 1995), 1–2.
14. Ibid., 9.
15. Ibid., 17.

16. See Peter L. Berger, *The Sacred Canopy: Elements of a Sociological Theory of Religion* (New York: Anchor Books, 1967), Part I, Chapter 1.

17. Tanner, *Theories of Culture*, 87.

18. William Leiss et al., *Social Communication in Advertising: Persons, Products, and Images of Well-Being* (London and New York: Routledge, 1997), 296.

19. Michael Schudson thinks that advertising may be influential as a type of religion because it subtly promotes images and attitudes, but it does not make the mistake of asking for belief. Schudson, *Advertising, the Uneasy Persuasion*, 226.

20. Durkheim states about the origin of religions: "Granted, if by origin one means an absolute first beginning, there is nothing scientific about the question, and it must resolutely be set aside." Durkheim, *The Elementary Forms of Religious Life*, 7.

21. I am indebted to my Princeton Theological Seminary colleague Ralph Lang for his previous input for this analysis.

22. Karl Marx, *Capital*, Volume 1 (Chicago: Charles H. Kerr & Company, 1912), 41.

23. Ibid., 42.

24. Ibid., 43.

25. Ibid.

26. Ibid., 44.

27. Sut Jhally, *The Codes of Advertising: Fetishism and the Political Economy of Meaning in the Consumer Society* (New York: Routledge, 1990), 27.

28. Ibid., 28–29.

29. Ibid., 29.

30. Ibid., 34.

31. Sut Jhally, *The Codes of Advertising: Fetishism and the Political Economy of Meaning in the Consumer Society* (New York: Routledge, 1990), 50.

32. Ibid.

33. Ibid., 53.

34. Ibid.

35. Ibid.

36. Ibid., 53–54.

37. Ibid., 54.

38. Ibid., 56.

39. See Gayatri Chakravorty Spivak's famous essay, "Can the Subaltern Speak?" *Marxism and the Interpretation of Cultures*, ed. Cary Nelson and Lawrence Grossberg (Urbana: University of Illinios Press, 1988) for an excellent postcolonial critique. I also recognize the "paternalism and racism" inherent in Durkheim's analysis of the aboriginal communities

in his analysis of totemism. Realizing this point of contention, I do not intend to propagate such oppressive structures in my own analysis.

40. Jhally, *The Codes of Advertising*, 53.
41. Ibid., 39.
42. Ibid., 45.
43. Ibid., 201.
44. Ibid., 195.
45. Ibid., 201.
46. Ibid., 202.
47. Ibid.
48. Jhally, "Advertising as Religion," 224.
49. Ibid., 225.
50. Ibid.
51. Ibid.
52. Ibid.
53. Ibid., 226.
54. Ibid.
55. Ibid., 227.
56. Ibid., 226.
57. Ibid., 226, 227.
58. Ibid.
59. Jhally, *The Codes of Advertising*, 196.
60. Ibid., 196–197.
61. Frederic Jameson, *Postmodernism, or The Cultural Logic of Late Capitalism* (Durham: Duke University Press, 1991), x.
62. Jhally, *The Codes of Advertising*, 49.
63. Ibid., 196.
64. James Twitchell, *Adcult USA: The Triumph of Advertising in American Culture* (New York: Columbia University Press, 1996), 11–12.
65. Leiss et al., *Social Communication in Advertising*, 70.
66. Grant McCracken, *Culture and Consumption: New Approaches to the Symbolic Character of Consumer Goods and Activities* (Bloomington: Indiana University Press, 1988), 118–129.
67. Ibid., 119.
68. Ibid., 123–124.
69. Leiss et al., *Social Communication in Advertising*, 45.
70. Mark Lewis Taylor, e-mail correspondence, March 11, 2005.
71. Jhally, "Advertising as Religion," 227.
72. Raymond Williams, "Advertising: The Magic System," in *Problems in Materialism and Culture* (London: New Left books, 1980), 185, as quoted in Jhally, "Advertising as Religion," 228.

73. In his video "Advertising and the End of the World," Jhally states that there are two kinds of questions that one may ask of advertising. The first one is: does an ad campaign for a product increase sales? This is the marketing question, and is of primary importance to companies. But Jhally says this is the wrong question. The second, and of course right question, is: what impact does advertising have on the culture? That is, what is its cultural role? What are the values articulated and expressed in the cultural field of society? Sut Jhally, *Advertising and the End of the World*, Video, written, edited, and produced by Sut Jhally (Distributed by Media Education Foundation, 1998).

74. Judith Williamson, *Decoding Advertisements: Ideology and Meaning in Advertising* (London: Marion Boyars, 1978), 47.

75. Jhally, "Advertising as Religion," 227.

76. Ibid., 199.

77. Ibid.

78. Ibid.

79. I am indebted to Mark Lewis Taylor for this example.

80. Mark Lewis Taylor, personal correspondence.

81. Juliet B. Schor, *The Overspent American: Why We Want What We Don't Need* (New York: HarperPerennial, 1998), 57.

82. Ibid.

83. Williamson, *Decoding Advertisements*, 46.

84. John Kavanaugh, *Following Christ in a Consumer Society*, 2nd ed. (Maryknoll, NY: Orbis Books, 1991), 26.

85. Jib Fowles, *Advertising and Popular Culture* (Thousand Oaks: Sage Publications, 1996), 40–41.

Chapter 2 Worshiping a Totem

1. Lukes, *Emile Durkheim*, 1, italics added.

2. Lukes, Chapter 25, "Durkheim and His Critics" especially Malinowski, van Gennep, and Radcliffe-Brown, ibid., 522–528. See also Claude Levi-Strauss, *Totemism*, trans. Rodney Needham (Boston: Beacon Press), 70–71, 95–97; Franco Ferrarotti, *Toward the Social Production of the Sacred: Durkheim, Weber, Freud* (La Jolla, CA.: Essay Press Inc., 1977), 9–30; and W.S.F. Pickering, *Durkheim's Sociology of Religion: Themes and Theories* (Boston: Routledge, 1984).

3. Lukes, *Emile Durkheim*, 31, 34. For instance, Lukes delineates three forms of argument that are problematic. First is the *petitio principii* in which Durkheim builds the argument into the premise in order to

provide for the conclusion. He does this most glaringly in his definition of religion. Second is the argument by elimination in which alternative explanations are presented only to be systematically discounted as Durkheim's "correct" theory unfolds. Last is Durkheim's treatment of evidence, wherein he ignores glaring facts that contradict his own work, such as clan societies without totems and vice versa.

4. Ibid., 34.

5. I do not intend to make a symmetrical correlation with Durkheim's theories and present society. Much of Durkheim's anthropological work has been shown to be rather "arm-chair" and has subsequently been disproven. Yet, let it be stated that Durkheim wrote at a time that was just beginning to see the rise of industrial capitalism, and certainly did not see advertising in the form that exists in the twenty–first century. What I seek to do is discover how his theories of religion and the sacred and profane may be useful in understanding certain present religious phenomena.

6. Pickering states that Durkheim never uses the phrase "deification of society" or "sacralization of society." It has been attributed to Durkheim by later scholars. See Pickering, *Durkheim's Sociology of Religion*, 234, 259–261.

7. Ralph Piddington as quoted in Ferrarotti, *Toward the Social Production of the Sacred*, 27–28.

8. Levi-Strauss, *Totemism*, 45.

9. Ibid., italics in original.

10. See Robert Bellah, "Introduction," in Emile Durkheim, *On Morality and Society* (Chicago: The University of Chicago Press, 1973), xviii.

11. Durkheim has often been accused of abolishing the individual or positing what may be thought of as "group think." But Bellah argues that this is not true as Durkheim saw "collective life [as] an emergent process of human action with its own systematic properties . . ." and he did not think that the social was of a "greater nor lesser ultimate reality than individual life." Ibid, xx.

12. Durkheim, *The Elementary Forms of Religious Life*, 13.

13. Ibid., 17. As Gianfranco Poggi states, this kind of "collective causality" makes for a very interesting argument and contribution to the sociology of knowledge. See Gianfranco Poggi, *Durkheim* (New York: Oxford University Press, 2000), 161.

14. Durkheim, *The Elementary Forms of Religious Life*, 17.

15. Ibid., 9. Levi-Strauss thinks Durkheim's explanation is "simplistic and reduces itself to an untenable attempt at monocausal explanation." That is, Levi-Strauss sees Durkheim's theories concerning the categories as functionalist. See Levi-Strauss, *Totemism*, 95–97 and Ferrarotti,

Toward the Social Production of the Sacred, 28–29. See also Lukes and his analysis concerning the categories, *Emile Durkheim,* 436–445.

16. Durkheim, *The Elementary Forms of Religious Life,* 7.
17. Ibid., 4.
18. Ibid., 24.
19. Ibid., 27.
20. Ibid., 34.
21. Ibid.
22. Ibid., 37.
23. Ibid., 38.
24. Ibid., 41.
25. Ibid., 42.
26. Ibid., 44. Italics in original.
27. Ibid.
28. Ibid.
29. Ibid.
30. Ibid.
31. Another reason that it is problematic, or at least intriguing, is Durkheim associated society with the sacred and the individual with the profane. Of course, the individual as he or she exists in society is one of the main topics for anthropology and sociology and has been taken up by such scholars as Mary Douglas, Thomas Luckmann, and Steven Lukes. For a good discussion of this aspect of Durkheim's work see Pickering, *Durkheim's Sociology of Religion,* 122–124. Also, one scholar in the tradition of Durkheim is Mircea Eliade. See his *The Sacred and the Profane: The Nature of Religion* (New York: Harcourt, Brace & World, Inc., 1959).
32. Pickering, *Durkheim's Sociology of Religion,* 147. Pickering does an excellent job of outlining the various critics and their arguments concerning the sacred and profane dichotomy. See especially, Part II, Chapter 8.
33. Poggi, *Durkheim,* 147–148.
34. Ibid., 147.
35. Colleen McDannell, *Material Christianity: Religion and Popular Culture in America* (New Haven & London: Yale University Press, 1995), 4.
36. Ibid., 5.
37. Durkheim, *The Elementary Forms of Religious Life,* 85–88.
38. Ibid., 85.
39. Ibid., 88. Durkheim's texts for analysis are Sir Baldwin Spencer and Francis James Gillen, *The Native Tribes of Central Australia* (London: Macmillan, 1899) and Sir Baldwin Spencer and Francis James Gillen, *The Northern Tribes of Central Australia* (London: Macmillan, 1904).
40. Durkheim, *The Elementary Forms of Religious Life,* 104, 105.
41. Ibid., 111.
42. Ibid., 114.

43. Ibid., 118.
44. Ibid.
45. Ibid., 127.
46. Ibid., 133.
47. Ibid.
48. Ibid.
49. Ibid., 133, 138.
50. Ibid., 150.
51. Ibid., 191.
52. Ibid.
53. Ibid., 192.
54. Ibid., 208.
55. Ibid.
56. Pickering, *Durkheim's Sociology of Religion*, 232.
57. Durkheim, *The Elementary Forms of Religious Life*, 236. Pickering states that Durkheim adapts Kant's moral argument for the existence of God: "[S]ince God does not exist and society does and since a moral authority is needed, society is precisely authority formerly supplied by God."
58. Ibid., 209.
59. Ibid. One might notice that at this point Durkheim has moved from Spencer and Gillen's world of totemism to his contemporary French society to prove how god and society are one and the same, and to support his idea of the sacred and the profane. Also, it is important to note that consumer society and/or capitalism assumes and relies on the promotion of individual self-interest for its success.
60. Ibid., 213.
61. Ibid., 214.
62. Ibid., 215.
63. Ibid., 222.
64. Ibid.
65. Ibid., 226–227.
66. Durkheim does recognize, however, that this theory of religion may still seem delusional. He asks, "By what other name can one call the state in which men find themselves when, as a great result of collective effervescence, they believe they have been swept up into a world entirely different from the one they have before their eyes?" Ibid., 227–228.
67. Ibid., 230. Italics in original.
68. Berger, *The Sacred Canopy*, 8–12.
69. Ibid., 9.
70. Roland Marchand, *Advertising the American Dream: Making Way for Modernity, 1920–1940* (Berkeley: University of California Press, 1985), 303.
71. Durkheim, *The Elementary Forms of Religious Life*, 419–420. Italics added.

72. Schudson, *Advertising, the Uneasy Persuasion*, 159.
73. Ibid.
74. Indeed, my questions are/were also Durkheim's questions. That is, one of the reasons he wrote *Forms* was to try and discern how it is that society sustains itself.
75. Poggi, *Durkheim*, 167.

Chapter 3   Locating Religious Dimensions

Portions of this chapter were first published as a supplementary article, "Advertising" by Tricia Sheffield in *Religion and American Cultures: An Encyclopedia of Traditions, Diversity, and Popular Expressions*, Volume 2, ed. Gary Laderman and Luis Leon (Santa Barbara, CA: ABC-CLIO, 2003), 445–446. Specifically see pages 70–71, 75–76, and 78.

1. Some excellent studies of the history of advertising in America are Stephen Fox, *The Mirror Makers: A History of American Advertising and Its Creators* (Chicago: University of Illinois Press, 1984); Jackson Lears, *Fables of Abundance: A Cultural History of Advertising in America* (New York: Basic Books, 1994); Leach, *Land of Desire*; Juliann Sivulka, *Soap, Sex, and Cigarettes: A Cultural History of American Advertising* (Belmont, CA.: Wadsworth Publishing Company, 1998); and Marchand, *Advertising the American Dream*.
2. T.J. Jackson Lears, "From Salvation to Self-Realization: Advertising and the Therapeutic Roots of the Consumer Culture, 1880–1930," in *The Culture of Consumption*, ed. Richard Wightman Fox and T.J. Jackson Lears (New York: Pantheon Books, 1983), 4.
3. Leach, *Land of Desire*, passim.
4. Schudson, *Advertising, the Uneasy Persuasion*, xiii.
5. Jerry Kirkpatrick, *In Defense of Advertising* (Westport: Quorum Books, 1994), 153–154.
6. Kavanaugh, *Following Christ in a Consumer Society*, 226.
7. Durkheim, *The Elementary Forms of Religious Life*, 208.
8. I agree with Jackson Lears, "From Salvation to Self-Realization," 20, in his nuanced critique of the role of consumer as easily manipulated:

[I] do not mean to endorse uncritically a liberal view of human nature as essentially rational and autonomous. On the contrary. Advertisers' growing recognition of human irrationality was a pale reflection of the most profound intellectual currents of the age: a recovery of the unconscious pioneered by Freud and Jung, a revolt against positivism led by James and Bergson, a broad questioning of the complacent liberal faith in human reason and progress. The problem was that manipulative advertisers distorted this critique of bourgeois culture beyond recognition. Emphasizing human irrationality, they used that emphasis to limit rather than deepen understanding of the human condition—to reject human freedom, rather than acknowledging its precariousness. Instead of transcending bourgeois culture, manipulative advertisers (like early therapists) helped to revitalize and transform it, creating new modes of hegemony for new managerial elites in the coming era of corporate capitalism.

9. Jhally, "Advertising and the End of the World."
10. Lears, "From Salvation to Self-Realization," 6.
11. Ibid.
12. As Ewen and Ewen note, "to consume in its original *usage* (French), meant 'to take up completely, devour, waste, spend.' " In almost all of the original English usages, consume had a negative connotation. With the expansion of an international market, to consume took on a more neutral, and then increasingly positive, tone. Today, "most Americans refer to themselves (unconsciously) as consumers." See Stuart and Elizabeth Ewen, *Channels of Desire: Mass Images and the Shaping of American Consciousness* (Minneapolis: University of Minnesota Press, 1992), 31.
13. Leach, *Land of Desire*, xv.
14. Lears, *Fables of Abundance*, 138.
15. Ibid., 117.
16. Ibid., 10.
17. Ibid., 117.
18. Ibid., 120.
19. One would not want to suggest or assert a notion of an innocent America, a country devoid of class, race, and gender oppression. Of course, any country that is founded on free land, free labor, and free capital will be marked by an imperialist, if not an oppressive, ideology. What was represented by early advertising was this kind of mythic abundance and simplicity as it was juxtaposed with the urbanization of the city. As more people moved from rural farm areas into industrial areas for job opportunities, many felt detached from the land as they crowded into burgeoning urban areas, and experienced "the anonymity of the city." See Lears, "From Salvation to Self-Realization," 6. Also, see Leach's ideas of nonconsensual consumerism above.
20. Leiss et al., *Social Communication in Advertising*, 57.
21. Stuart Ewen, *All Consuming Images: The Politics of Style in Contemporary Culture*, rev. ed. (New York: Basic Books, 1999), 71.
22. Ewen and Ewen, *Channels of Desire*, 29.

23. Lears, "From Salvation to Self-Realization," 10.
24. Ibid., 4.
25. Lears, *Fables of Abundance*, 139.
26. Sivulka, *Soap, Sex, and Cigarettes*, 50.
27. Ibid., 55.
28. Ibid., 53.
29. Lears, *Fables of Abundance*, 209.
30. Lears, "From Salvation to Self-Realization," 23.
31. Ibid., 30.
32. Leach, *Land of Desire*, 147.
33. Ibid., 146.
34. Christopher Lasch, *The Culture of Narcissism: American Life in An Age of Diminishing Expectations* (New York: Norton, 1979), passim.
35. Ibid., 72.
36. Jerry Kirkpatrick argues against the critics who attack advertising as an infringement on the human consciousness. He states, "This attack denies the volitional nature of reason, that is free will; consequently, it denies either explicitly or implicitly, the validity of human consciousness as such." Kirkpatrick, *In Defense of Advertising*, 3.
37. Gary Cross, *An All-Consuming Century: Why Commercialism Won in Modern America* (New York: Columbia University Press, 2000), 29.
38. Joseph Haroutunian, *Lust for Power* (New York: Scribner's Sons, 1949), 55–60.
39. Lears, *Fables of Abundance*, 154.
40. Ibid.
41. As quoted in Cross, *An All-Consuming Century*, 51.
42. Reason-why copywriters were John E. Kennedy, Claude Hopkins, Albert Lasker, and Helen Resor. Sivulka, *Soap, Sex, and Cigarettes*, 107.
43. Lears, "From Salvation to Self-Realization," 18.
44. Impressionistic advertising copywriters were J. Walter Thompson Agency, Theodore MacManus, and Raymond Rubicam. Sivulka, *Soap, Sex, and Cigarettes*, 113.
45. Ibid. Sivulka also tells us that the two schools of advertising theory existed at the same time together for a short while. Usually, the object that was being advertised dictated the kind of copy. See also 115.
46. Cross asserts, "And most of the time, the goods that asserted status also had nonsocial meaning and appeals—control over nature, freedom from the past, or simply individual pleasure in feel, taste, and comfort. The secret success of consumerism was that these messages to self and others were so layered, complex, and hidden." Cross, *An All-Consuming Century*, 22.

47. Ibid., 21.
48. Marchand, *Advertising the American Dream*, 335.
49. Ibid., 348.
50. Sivulka, *Soap, Sex, and Cigarettes*, 148.
51. Marchand, *Advertising the American Dream*, 264.
52. Ibid., 166.
53. Williamson, *Decoding Advertisements*, 47.
54. Marchand, *Advertising the American Dream*, 167.
55. Cross, *An All-Consuming Century*, 22.
56. Ibid., 3.
57. Ibid., 35.
58. "Printers' Ink," November 7, 1929, as quoted in Sivulka, *Soap, Sex, and Cigarettes*, 150.
59. Marchand, *Advertising the American Dream*, 169.
60. Marchand, *Advertising the American Dream*, 170.
61. Ibid., 171–172.
62. Ibid., 151.
63. Marchand, *Advertising the American Dream*, 187.
64. Ibid., 188. Italics added.
65. Ibid., 264. Italics in original.
66. "Printers' Ink Monthly" March, 1926 as quoted in Marchand, *Advertising the American Dream*, 265.
67. Marchand, *Advertising the American Dream*, 264–265.
68. Ibid., 265.
69. Ibid., 267.
70. Ibid., 269.
71. Ibid., 274. For an outstanding study of the intersection between advertising and American (religious) holidays, see Leigh Eric Schmidt, *Consumer Rites: The Buying and Selling of American Holidays* (Princeton: Princeton University Press, 1995).
72. Ibid., *Advertising the American Dream*, 276.
73. Ibid., 273.
74. Ibid. Italics added.
75. Ibid., 276.
76. Ibid., 335.
77. Ibid., 282.
78. Sivulka, *Soap, Sex, and Cigarettes*, 199.
79. Ibid., 205.
80. Ibid., 201.
81. Cross, *An All-Consuming Century*, 71.
82. Ibid., 67. This same attitude was also prevalent during World War II.

83. Ibid., 134. Cross notes that "They [advertisers] redefined freedom to mean not civil liberty or the right to work, but the ability to find identity in the choice of goods to buy."

84. Ibid., 124.

85. Sivulka, *Soap, Sex, and Cigarettes*, 219.

86. Ibid., 218–219.

87. An excellent study of the history of radio is Michelle Hilmes, *Radio Voices: American Broadcasting, 1922–1952* (Minneapolis: University of Minnesota Press, 1997).

88. Sivulka, *Soap, Sex, and Cigarettes*, 223.

89. Ibid., 230–231.

90. Ibid., 232.

91. Ibid.

92. Ibid.

93. Cross, *An All-Consuming Century*, 111.

94. Ibid.

95. Ibid., 112.

96. Sivulka, *Soap, Sex, and Cigarettes*, 240.

97. Ibid., 243.

98. Ibid., 245.

99. Fox, *The Mirror Makers*, 179.

100. Ibid., 178.

101. Ibid., 210.

102. Sivulka, *Soap, Sex, and Cigarettes*, 272.

103. Fox, *The Mirror Makers*, 217.

104. Sivulka, *Soap, Sex, and Cigarettes*, 253.

105. Ibid.

106. Ibid., 254, 255.

107. Cross, *An All-Consuming Century*, 152.

108. Fox, *The Mirror Makers*, 184.

109. Ibid., 187.

110. Ibid., 200.

111. Ibid., 179, 180.

112. Sivulka, *Soap, Sex, and Cigarettes*, 265.

113. Fox, *The Mirror Makers*, 179.

114. Ibid., 231.

115. Sivulka, *Soap, Sex, and Cigarettes*, 263.

116. Ibid.

117. Ibid., 281.

118. Ibid., 316.

119. Ibid., 290.

120. Fox, *The Mirror Makers*, 280.

121. Sivulka, *Soap, Sex, and Cigarettes*, 302.
122. Ibid., 304.
123. Cross, *An All-Consuming Century*, 178.
124. Sivulka, *Soap, Sex, and Cigarettes*, 308–309.
125. Cross, *An All-Consuming Century*, 167. We see the same phenomenon later in the 1990s when "grunge" and "hip-hop" fashions also get co-opted into mainstream consumerism. Italics in original.
126. Ibid.
127. Ibid., 181.
128. Sivulka, *Soap, Sex, and Cigarettes*, 325.
129. See "Fashion, Sexuality and Representation at the *Fin de Siecle*" and "Re-imaging the Feminine: Fashion, Modernity and Identity in Britain between the Wars," in Cheryl Buckley and Hilary Fawcett, *Fashioning the Feminine: Representation and Women's Fashion from the Fin de Siecle to the Present* (London and New York: I.B. Tauris Publishers, 2002).
130. Sivulka, *Soap, Sex, and Cigarettes*, 323.
131. Fox, *The Mirror Makers*, 299.
132. Betty Friedan, *The Feminine Mystique* (New York: Dell Publishing Co., 1974).
133. Cross, *An All-Consuming Century*, 155.
134. Ibid., 163.
135. Fox, *The Mirror Makers*, 328.
136. Sivulka, *Soap, Sex, and Cigarettes*, 356.
137. Ibid.
138. Ibid., 337.
139. Cross, *An All-Consuming Century*, 215.
140. Sivulka, *Soap, Sex, and Cigarettes*, 367.
141. Ibid., 366.
142. Ibid., 373.
143. Andrew Wernick, *Promotional Culture: Advertising, Ideology, and Symbolic Expression* (London: Sage Publications, 1991), 49.
144. Julie Baumgold, "The Brad and the Beautiful," in *Vogue*, November 1997.
145. Cross, *An All-Consuming Century*, 202.
146. Ibid., 193.
147. Sacvan Bercovitch, *The American Jeremiad* (Madison: University of Wisconsin Press, 1978).
148. Sivulka, *Soap, Sex, and Cigarettes*, 380.
149. This era saw the advent of Generation X. This was a new cynical consumer who was concerned less with image and more with reliability and durability in a product. Generation Xers were anti-fashion or interested in hip-hop chic as fostered by the emerging rap music

world. They were consumers who demanded that advertising be honest and simple. And of course, advertising co-opted their anticonformist stance much like in the 1960s. Ibid., 389, 390.
150. Ibid., 360.
151. Ibid.
152. Ibid., 361.
153. Ibid., 405.
154. Theresa Howard, "Hubcap Ads Put New Spin on Marketing," in www. keepmedia.com/pubs/USATODAY/2004.07/19.
155. Ibid.
156. Sivulka, *Soap, Sex, and Cigarettes*, 380.
157. Leiss et al., *Social Communication in Advertising*, 51.
158. See Schmidt, *Consumer Rites*, esp. 105–191.
159. Guy Debord, *The Society of the Spectacle* (New York: Zone Books, 1995), 12.
160. Jameson, *Postmodernism*, 275.
161. Jean Baudrillard, *The System of Objects*, trans. James Benedict (London: Verso, 1996), 194.
162. Cross, *An All-Consuming Century*, 236.
163. Sivulka, *Soap, Sex, and Cigarettes*, 397. One person was reported to have said to a young boy: "If you want to play basketball well, then buy Reeboks. If you just want to look good, then buy Nikes." Personal conversation with family member.
164. *Adbusters* May/June 2001 (Volume 9, Number 35), 83.
165. Ruth La Ferla, "Wearing Their Beliefs on Their Chests," in the *New York Times*, March 29, 2005. I am grateful to Monica Ager for suggesting this article to me.
166. Cross, *An All-Consuming Century*, 236.
167. Ibid., 248.
168. Ibid.
169. Naomi Klein, *No Logo: Taking Aim at the Brand Bullies* (New York: St. Martin's Press, 1999), 90.
170. Ibid., 89.
171. It is estimated that "a billion dollars will be spent on product placement in the United States" in 2005. Ken Auletta, "The New Pitch: Do Ads Still Work," in *The New Yorker*, March 28, 2005, 38.
172. I am indebted to Catherine Keller for suggesting this movie to me.
173. First, there have been worldwide counterculture protests at the G-8 Summit meetings and the rise of anarchist demonstrations against the consumer culture. Second, there is a trend in some affluent, middle-class communities to voluntarily downshift one's spending in order to be more fiscally responsible and environmentally sound. Third, Kalle

Lasn leads an organization of "culture jammers" called *Adbusters* in which they use advertising in an ironic manner to expose the so-called evils of corporate capitalism and the branding of America. See Sivulka, *Soap, Sex, and Cigarettes*, 396–397; Schor, *The Overspent American*; Kalle Lasn, *Culture Jam: The Uncooling of America*^{TM} (New York: Eagle Brook, 1999).
174. Cross, *An All-Consuming Century*, 242.
175. Ibid., 239.
176. http://www.whitehouse.gov/news/releases/2001/10/20011011–7.html.
177. Sivulka, *Soap, Sex, and Cigarettes*, 428. Italics added.

Chapter 4 Religious Dimensions of Advertising

1. See chapter 2 with regard to Durkheim and his critics.
2. Wayne Proudfoot, *Religious Experience* (Berkeley: University of California Press, 1985), 196.
3. Ibid., 197.
4. Ibid.
5. John B. Cobb, Jr., *Postmodernism and Public Policy: Reframing Religion, Culture, Education, Sexuality, Class, Race, Politics, and the Economy* (Albany: State University of New York Press, 2002), 122–123.
6. John B. Cobb, Jr., *Sustaining the Common Good: A Christian Perspective on the Global Economy* (Cleveland, OH.: The Pilgrim Press, 1994), 13–14.
7. Ibid., 33–34.
8. Ibid., 11.
9. Schudson, *Advertising, the Uneasy Persuasion*, 224.
10. Tillich, *Systematic Theology*, Volume 1, 216.
11. Ibid.
12. Cobb, *Sustaining the Common Good*, 28.
13. Adbusters Media Foundation, *New York Times*, July 3, 2003.
14. Mark Taylor asserts, "[r]arely does Tillich fail to provoke and equip us in some ways for reflecting on, and acting in relation to, the distinctive problems we discern, even if, finally, this may mean rendering negative judgments about Tillich's work." Mark Kline Taylor, *Paul Tillich: Theologian of the Boundaries* (Minneapolis: Fortress Press, 1991), 12.
15. See John B. Cobb, Jr. and Herman E. Daly, *For the Common Good: Redirecting the Economy toward Community, the Environment, and a*

Sustainable Future, 2nd ed. (Boston: Beacon Press, 1994); Cobb, Jr., *Sustaining the Common Good*; Sallie McFague, *Life Abundant: Rethinking Theology and Economy for a Planet in Peril* (Minneapolis: Fortress Press, 2001); M. Douglas Meeks, *God the Economist: The Doctrine of God and Political Economy* (Minneapolis: Fortress Press, 1989); and Mark Kline Taylor, *Remembering Esperanza: A Cultural–Political Theology for North American Praxis* (Maryknoll, NY: Orbis Books, 1990).

16. Tanner, *Theories of Culture*, 87.
17. John Macquarrie, *Mediators between Human and Divine: From Moses to Muhammad* (New York: Continuum, 1996).
18. Ibid., 11.
19. Tillich, *Systematic Theology*, Volume 1, 121.
20. Paul Tillich, *Systematic Theology*, Volume 2 (Chicago: The University of Chicago Press, 1957), 93.
21. Ibid.
22. Ibid., 169.
23. Ibid.
24. Ibid.
25. Ibid.
26. One might assert this as a capitalist atonement theory.
27. Paul Tillich, "Aspects of a Religious Analysis of Culture," in *Theology of Culture*, ed. Robert C. Kimball (New York: Oxford University Press, 1964), 46.
28. Paul Tillich, *Systematic Theology*, Volume 3 (Chicago: The University of Chicago Press, 1963), 189.
29. In the tradition of Durkheim, sociologist Peter Berger also recognizes this cultural phenomenon.
30. Tillich, *Systematic Theology*, Volume 3, 189.
31. Baudrillard calls this the "presumption of collectivity." This is a consumption process whereby the individual believes that he or she is buying a product that will differentiate oneself from other people, but, in fact, everyone is purchasing the same product. The purchase is actually a "regressive identification with a vague collective totality, and hence an internalization of the sanction of the social group." Baudrillard, *The System of Objects*, 178, 179–180. See also Judith Butler, "Performative Acts and Gender Constitution: An Essay in Phenomenology and Feminist Theory," in *Performing Feminisms: Feminist Critical Theory and Theatre*, ed. Sue-Ellen Case (Baltimore: Johns Hopkins University Press, 1990), 272.
32. McFague, *Life Abundant*, 93.
33. Ibid., 96.

34. Ibid. According to an article in *The New Yorker*, the United States spent "more than five hundred billion dollars" on advertising in 2004, "half the world-wide total." Auletta, "The New Pitch," 34.
35. McFague, *Life Abundant*, 97.
36. Meeks, *God the Economist*, 158–162.
37. Ibid., 160.
38. Meeks lists three concepts of God that support human desires as coded into needs: "Divine aseity and the liberty of the independent human being, divine sovereignty and needs as necessity, divine infinity and human insatiability." Ibid., 162–170.
39. Ibid., 158.
40. Ibid.
41. Harvard economist Juliet Schor does an extensive study of the conflation of needs with desires in the Unites States and how some people are choosing to "downsize" in response to the "tyranny of the Joneses." See *The Overspent American*.
42. Meeks, *God the Economist*, 161. See also Cobb, *Sustaining the Common Good*, 33.
43. Meeks, *God the Economist*, 161.
44. Ibid.
45. Ibid., 162.
46. Ibid., 168.
47. Cobb, *Sustaining the Common Good*, 56–57.
48. Meeks, *God the Economist*, 169.
49. Franz J. Hinkelammert, *The Ideological Weapons of Death: A Theological Critique of Capitalism* (Maryknoll, NY: Orbis Books, 1986), 15, as quoted in Meeks, *God the Economist*, 169, italics added.
50. See chapter 2.
51. See my analysis of the American Thanksgiving shopping ritual in chapter 3.
52. Italics added.
53. Baudrillard, *The System of Objects*, 173.
54. Meeks, *God the Economist*, 173.
55. Ibid., 172.
56. Kavanaugh, *Following Christ in a Consumer Society*, 26, as quoted in Meeks, *God the Economist*, 170.
57. McFague, *Life Abundant*, 97.
58. Ibid., 94.
59. Ibid., 95.
60. Meeks, *God the Economist*, 170–171.
61. Ibid., 171.
62. Ibid.

63. Ibid.
64. Ibid., 172.
65. Cobb, *Postmodernism and Public Policy*, 103.
66. McFague, *Life Abundant*, 97.
67. Meeks, *God the Economist*, 174.
68. Ibid., 177.
69. Ibid., 180.
70. Ibid., 173.
71. Durkheim, *The Elementary Forms of Religious Life*, 133.
72. In no way is this argument meant to diminish or trivialize the faith of Christians and their understanding of the Eucharist or Lord's Supper. My argument is that advertising contains religious dimensions, and one of these dimensions is a form of sacramentality akin to the Christian understanding of sacrament. In the culture of consumer capitalism, things have become sacred, and do tend to have a type of religious symbol since the ultimate concern of our society is the maintenance of market capitalism.
73. Mark C. Taylor, *About Religion: Economies of Faith in Virtual Culture* (Chicago: University of Chicago Press, 1999), 5, italics added.
74. Thorstein Veblen, *The Theory of the Leisure Class* (New York: Penguin Books, 1994), 25–26.
75. Ibid., 29.
76. McDannell, *Material Christianity*, 19.
77. Tillich, *Systematic Theology*, Volume 3, 120. See also his lecture "Nature and Sacrament," in Taylor, *Paul Tillich*, 82–95.
78. Tillich, *Systematic Theology*, Volume 3, 120.
79. Ibid, 125.
80. Ibid., 122.
81. Ibid., 124.
82. McFague, *Life Abundant*, 99–123.
83. Taylor, *Remembering Esperanza*, 234–235.
84. McFague, *Life Abundant*, 173.
85. John Dominic Crossan, *Jesus: A Revolutionary Biography* (San Francisco: HarperSanFrancisco, 1994), 73–74 as quoted in McFague, *Life Abundant*, 175.
86. McFague, *Life Abundant*, 174.
87. Ibid.
88. Ibid., 175.
89. Ibid., 174.
90. Mark McClain Taylor, "Tracking Spirit: Theology as Cultural Critique in the Americas," in *Changing Conversations: Religious Reflection and*

Cultural Analysis, ed. Sheila Greeve Davaney and Dwight N. Hopkins (New York and London: Routledge, 1997), 135.
91. Ibid., 134.
92. Taylor, *Remembering Esperanza*, 233. Also see chapter 3 concerning the difference between the material and materialism.
93. Ibid., 234.
94. Ibid., 238.
95. Ibid., 240.
96. Tillich, *Systematic Theology*, Volume 3, 349.
97. Tillich, *Systematic Theology*, Volume 1, 211.
98. "Jesus answered, 'The first is, "Hear, O Israel: the Lord our God, the Lord is One."'" *The New Oxford Annotated Bible*, New Revised Standard Version, ed. Bruce M. Metzger and Roland E. Murphy (New York: Oxford University Press, 1991).
99. Tillich, *Systematic Theology*, Volume 1, 12, italics in original.
100. Ibid., 1, 14, italics in original.
101. Although he does add later that "God is . . . the name for that which concerns man ultimately." Ibid., 211.
102. Ibid., 14.
103. Ibid., 50.
104. Ibid., 48.
105. Ibid., 211.
106. Ibid., 215.
107. Ibid., 216. This argument may also be applied to advertising as sacramentality.
108. Tillich, *Systematic Theology*, Volume 2, 116.
109. Ibid.
110. Tillich, *Systematic Theology*, Volume 3, 130.
111. Durkheim, *The Elementary Forms of Religious Life*, 2.
112. Ibid.
113. Tillich, *Systematic Theology*, Volume 1, 218.
114. Tillich, "Aspects of a Religious Analysis of Culture," 41.
115. Ibid.
116. Tillich, *Systematic Theology*, Volume 1, 217–218. Tillich seems to collapse the two categories of holy and secular in much the same way as Durkheim envelopes the sacred and profane. Tillich's binary does not seem to be a true one of parity. However, he does, unlike Durkheim, recognize that religion or the holy contains things that are also secular. See chapter 2, Poggi's critique.
117. Ibid., 221.
118. Ibid.
119. Ibid.

120. Ibid., 273.
121. Tillich, "Aspects of a Religious Analysis of Culture," 42.
122. See also Paul Tillich, "Religon and Secular Culture," in Taylor, *Paul Tillich*, 119–126.
123. Cobb, *Sustaining the Common Good*, 49.
124. Ibid., 49.
125. Ibid., 28.
126. Ibid., 46.
127. Mark Lewis Taylor, e-mail correspondence, March 11, 2005.
128. Although Cobb does believe that earthism is the best alternative to the ideology of growth, as a Christian theologian he cannot give full support to this theory since he does not believe that the earth is God. Cobb, *Sustaining the Common Good*, 40.
129. Ibid., 61.
130. Ibid., 67.
131. For an insightful critique of Nike's unfair labor practices see Cynthia Enloe, "The Globetrotting Sneaker," in *Ms.*, March/April 1995, 10–15.
132. Cobb, *Sustaining the Common Good*, xii, 44.
133. Ibid., 65.
134. Ibid., 130–131.

Chapter 5 Disruptive Performative Identities

Portions of this chapter were first published as "Cover Girls: Toward a Theory of Female Divine Embodiment," in *The Journal of Religion and Society*, Volume 4, ed. Ronald Simkins (Omaha, Nebraska: Creighton University, 2002). Author copyright.

1. Jhally, "Advertising as Religion," 229.
2. Schor, *The Overspent American*, 57.
3. Cross, *An All-Consuming Century*, 2.
4. Ibid., 238–239.
5. Ibid., 12.
6. Ibid., 16.
7. Butler, "Performative Acts and Gender Constitution," 281.
8. Michel de Certeau, *The Practice of Everyday Life* (Berkeley: University of California Press, 1984).

9. John Storey, *Cultural Consumption and Everyday Life* (London: Arnold Books), 136.

10. Ibid., 129.

11. Ibid.

12. Ibid., 130.

13. Michel Maffesoli, *The Time of the Tribes: The Decline of Individualism in Mass Society* (London: Sage, 1996), 98.

14. Maffesoli also uses Durkheim's theories of religion as a hermeneutic principle. Ibid., 21.

15. Ibid., 25, 140.

16. See Juliet B. Schor and Douglas B. Holt, eds., *The Consumer Society Reader* (New York: The New Press, 2000), x–xxii.

17. Ibid., x.

18. Ibid., xii.

19. Ibid.

20. I have noted some of Baudrillard's theories of advertising throughout the book.

21. Schor and Holt, *The Consumer Society Reader*, xvii.

22. Ibid., xix.

23. Durkheim, *The Elementary Forms of Religious Life*, 222.

24. Paul Tillich, "The Nature of Religious Language," in *Theology of Culture*, ed. Robert C. Kimball (New York: Oxford University Press, 1964), 55.

25. Ibid., 54.

26. Peter Berger, *The Sacred Canopy*, 9.

27. Tillich, "Aspects of a Religious Analysis of Culture," in *Theology of Culture*, 42.

28. Mary McClintock Fulkerson, *Changing the Subject: Women's Discourses and Feminist Theology* (Minneapolis: Fortress Press, 1994), 73.

29. Michel Foucault, *Language, Counter-Memory, Practice: Selected Essays and Interviews*, ed. Donald Bouchard (Oxford: Blackwell, 1977) as quoted in Elizabeth Grosz, *Volatile Bodies: Toward a Corporeal Feminism* (Bloomington and Indianapolis: Indiana University Press, 1994), 146.

30. Foucault, *Language, Counter-Memory, Practice* and *The History of Sexuality: Volume 1, An Introduction*, trans. Robert Hurley (London: Allen Lane, 1978).

31. Grosz, *Volatile Bodies*, 147.

32. Michel Foucault, *Discipline and Punish: The Birth of the Prison* (New York: Pantheon, 1977), 92–93.

33. Jana Sawicki, *Disciplining Foucault: Feminism, Power, and the Body* (New York and London: Routledge, 1991), 11.

34. Sandra Lee Bartky, *Femininity and Domination: Studies in the Phenomenology of Oppression* (New York and London: Routledge, 1990), 65.

35. For background of the "male gaze," I am drawing on Jean-Paul Sartre's analysis of the "Look" in *Being and Nothingness*. Here he describes looking through a keyhole uninterrupted or watched. But suddenly, he is aware that someone is looking at him watch another. His behavior modifies his entire being, and he is aware that he has been modified. This awareness is what Sartre calls "shame" in recognizing that he is indeed the object which the Other is looking at and judging. The Other, then, is he who sees without being seen and he is the only real "I" from which all others are merely others with a small "o." According to Simone de Beauvoir, the Other then becomes the Subject, and the One, and the sexed female becomes the Other as incidental, or inessential. Woman is defined and differentiated according to man. This is important for the male gaze embodied in the female. A woman is aware that the gaze makes one an object and strips one of freedom, yet when one looks at other women, it is often with the same lens of the male gaze that one perceives the self as an incarnated being, and subsequently denies one's own subjectivity. See Jean-Paul Sartre, *Being and Nothingness*, trans. Hazel E. Barnes (New York: Philosophical Library, 1956); Simone De Beauvoir *The Second Sex*, trans. H.M. Parshley (New York: Bantam Books, 1952); and Stephen Melville, "Division of the Gaze, or Remarks on the Color and Tenor of Contemporary 'Theory,' " in *Vision in Context: Historical and Contemporary Perspectives on Sight*, ed. Teresa Brennan and Martin Jay (New York: Routledge, 1996), 101–116.

36. Erving Goffman, *Gender Advertisements* (New York: Harper and Row, 1979), 25.

37. Foucault, *Discipline and Punish*, 201.

38. Bartky, *Femininity and Domination*, 65.

39. Foucault, *Discipline and Punish*, 208.

40. Bartky, *Femininity and Domination*, 80.

41. Ibid., 72.

42. Ibid., 80.

43. Rosi Braidotti, *Nomadic Subjects: Embodiment and Sexual Difference in Contemporary Feminist Theory* (New York: Columbia University Press, 1994), 199.

44. bell hooks states, "Not only will I stare. I want my look to change reality. Even in the worst circumstances of domination, the ability to manipulate one's gaze in the face of structures of domination that would contain it, opens up the possibility of agency." bell hooks, *Black Looks: Race and Representation* (Boston: South End Press, 1992), 116.

45. Luce Irigaray, *This Sex Which Is Not One*, trans. Catherine Porter with Carolyn Burke (Ithaca: Cornell University Press, 1985), 76.

46. Luce Irigaray, *Speculum of the Other Woman*, trans. Gillian C. Gill (Ithaca: Cornell University Press, 1985). See also Diana Fuss, *Essentially Speaking: Feminism, Nature and Difference* (New York: Routledge, 1989) for a good explanation of Irigaray's theories.

47. John Berger, *Ways of Seeing* (London: British Broadcasting Corporation and Penguin, 1972), 51.

48. Marchand, *Advertising the American Dream*, 176.

49. Ibid.

50. Ibid.

51. Luce Irigaray, *I Love to You: Sketch of a Possible Felicity in History*, trans. Alison Martin (New York: Routledge, 1996), 60.

52. Braidotti, *Nomadic Subjects*, 98, 99.

53. Ibid., 98.

54. Ibid., 98, 99.

55. Ibid., 199. Braidotti defines materialism as an emphasis on the "embodied and sexually differentiated structure of the speaking subject."

56. Annette Kuhn, *Powers of the Image: Essays on Representation and Sexuality* (New York: Routledge, 1985) as quoted in hooks, *Black Looks*, 122–123.

57. Ann Friedberg, "A Denial of Difference: Theories of Cinematic Identification," in *Psychoanalysis and Cinema*, ed. E. Ann Kaplan (New York: Routledge, 1990) as quoted in hooks, *Black Looks*, 119.

58. Stuart Hall, as quoted in hooks, *Black Looks*, 131. No bibliographic citation provided.

59. Butler, "Performative Acts and Gender Constitution," 271.

60. Ibid., 272.

61. Ibid., 271. Italics added.

62. Ibid., 273.

63. See Tillich's definition above.

64. Williamson, *Decoding Advertisements*, 46.

65. Cobb, Jr., *Sustaining the Common Good*, 61.

Bibliography

Auletta, Ken, "The New Pitch: Do Ads Still Work?" in *The New Yorker*, March 28, 2005.

Bartky, Sandra Lee. *Femininity and Domination: Studies in the Phenomenology of Oppression*. New York and London: Routledge: 1990.

Baudrillard, Jean. *The System of Objects*, trans. James Benedict. London: Verso, 1996.

Baumgold, Julie, "The Brad and the Beautiful," in *Vogue*, November 1997.

Bercovitch, Sacvan. *The American Jeremiad*. Madison: University of Wisconsin Press, 1978.

Berger, John. *Ways of Seeing*. London: British Broadcasting Corporation and Penguin, 1972.

Berger, Peter. *The Sacred Canopy: Elements of a Sociological Theory of Religion*. New York: Anchor Books, 1967.

Braidotti, Rosi. *Nomadic Subjects: Embodiment and Sexual Difference in Contemporary Feminist Theory*. New York: Columbia University Press, 1993.

Buckley, Cheryl and Hilary Fawcett. *Fashioning the Feminine: Representation and Women's Fashion from the Fin de Siecle to the Present*. London and New York: I.B. Tauris Publishers, 2002.

Butler, Judith. "Performative Acts and Gender Constitution: An Essay in Phenomenology and Feminist Theory," in *Performing Feminisms: Feminist Critical Theory and Theatre*, ed. Sue-Ellen Case. Baltimore: Johns Hopkins University Press, 1990.

Cobb, John B., Jr. *Postmodernism and Public Policy: Reframing Religion, Culture, Education, Sexuality, Class, Race, Politics, and the Economy*. Albany: State University of New York Press, 2002.

———. *Sustaining the Common Good: A Christian Perspective on the Global Economy*. Cleveland, OH: The Pilgrim Press, 1994.

Cobb, John B., Jr. and Herman E. Daly. *For the Common Good: Redirecting the Economy toward Community, the Environment, and a Sustainable Future*, 2nd ed. Boston: Beacon Press, 1994.

Cross, Gary. *An All-Consuming Century: Why Commercialism Won in Modern America*. New York: Columbia University Press, 2000.

Crossan, John Dominic. *Jesus: A Revolutionary Biography*. San Francisco: HarperSanfrancisco, 1994.

de Beauvoir, Simone. *The Second Sex*, trans. H.M. Parshley. New York: Bantam Books, 1952.

de Certeau, Michel. *The Practice of Everyday Life*. Berkeley: University of California Press, 1984.

Debord, Guy. *The Society of the Spectacle*. New York: Zone Books, 1995.

Durkheim, Emile. *The Elementary Forms of Religious Life*, new translation by Karen E. Fields. New York: The Free Press, 1995.

———. *On Morality and Society*, ed. Robert Bellah. Chicago: The University of Chicago Press, 1973.

Eliade, Mircea. *The Sacred and the Profane: The Nature of Religion*. New York: Harvest Books, 1959.

Enloe, Cynthia, "The Globetrotting Sneaker," in *Ms.*, March/April 1995.

Ewen, Stuart. *All Consuming Images: The Politics of Style in Contemporary Culture*, rev. ed. New York: Basic Books, 1999.

Ewen, Stuart and Elizabeth Ewen. *Channels of Desire: Mass Images and the Shaping of American Consciousness*. Minneapolis: University of Minnesota Press, 1992.

Ferrarotti, Franco. *Toward the Social Production of the Sacred: Durkheim, Weber, Freud*. La Jolla, CA.: Essay Press Inc., 1977.

Foucault, Michel. *The History of Sexuality, Volume 1, An Introduction*, trans. Robert Hurley. London: Allen Lane, 1978.

———. *Discipline and Punish: The Birth of the Prison*. New York: Pantheon Books, 1977.

———. *Language, Counter-Memory, Practice: Selected Essays and Interviews*, ed. Donald Bouchard. Oxford: Blackwell Publishing, 1977.

Fowles, Jib. *Advertising and Popular Culture*. Thousand Oaks, CA: Sage Publications, 1996.

Fox, Stephen. *The Mirror Makers: A History of American Advertising and Its Creators*. Chicago: University of Illinois Press, 1984.

Friedan, Betty. *The Feminine Mystique*. New York: Dell Publishing Company, 1974.

Friedberg, Ann, "A Denial of Difference: Theories of Cinematic Identification," in *Psychoanalysis and Cinema*, ed. E. Ann Kaplan. New York and London: Routledge, 1990.

Fulkerson, Mary McClintock. *Changing the Subject: Women's Discourses and Feminist Theology*. Minneapolis: Fortress Press, 1994.

Fuss, Diana. *Essentially Speaking: Feminism, Nature and Difference*. New York and London: Routledge, 1989.

Gans, Herbert J. *Popular Culture and High Culture: An Analysis of Evaluation and Taste*. New York: Basic Books, 1975.

Galbraith, John Kenneth. *The Affluent Society*, 40th anniversary edition. Boston: Houghton Mifflin Company, 1998.

Goffman, Erving. *Gender Advertisements*. New York: Harper & Row, 1979.

Grosz, Elizabeth. *Volatile Bodies: Toward a Corporeal Feminism*. Bloomington and Indianapolis: Indiana University Press, 1994.

Haroutunian, Joseph. *Lust for Power*. New York: Scribner's Sons, 1949.

Hilmes, Michelle. *Radio Voices: American Broadcasting, 1922–1952*. Minneapolis: University of Minnesota Press, 1997.

Hinkelammert, Franz J. *The Ideological Weapons of Death: A Theological Critique of Capitalism*. Maryknoll, NY: Orbis Books, 1986.

hooks, bell. *Black Looks: Race and Representation*. Boston: South End Press, 1992.

Howard, Theresa, "Hubcap Ads Put New Spin on Marketing." www.keepmedia.com/pubs/USATODAY/2004.07/19.

Irigaray, Luce. *I Love to You: Sketch of a Possible Felicity in History*, trans. Alison Martin. New York and London: Routledge, 1996.

―――. *Speculum of the Other Woman*, trans. Gillian C. Gill. Ithaca: Cornell University Press, 1985.

―――. *This Sex Which Is Not One*, trans. Catherine Porter with Carolyn Burke. Ithaca: Cornell University Press, 1985.

Jameson, Frederic. *Postmodernism, or the Cultural Logic of Late Capitalism*. Durham: Duke University Press, 1991.

Jhally, Sut. *Advertising and the End of the World*. Video. Written, edited, and produced by Sut Jhally. Distributed by Media Education Foundation, 1998.

―――. "Advertising as Religion: The Dialectic and Technology of Magic," in *Cultural Politics in Contemporary America*, ed. Ian Angus and Sut Jhally. New York and London: Routledge, 1989.

―――. *The Codes of Advertising: Fetishism and the Political Economy of Meaning in Consumer Society*. New York: St. Martin's Press, 1987.

Kavanaugh, John. *Following Christ in a Consumer Society: The Spirituality of Cultural Resistance*, rev. ed. Maryknoll, NY: Orbis Books, 1991.

Kirkpatrick, Jerry. *In Defense of Advertising: Arguments from Reason, Ethical Egoism, and Laissez-Faire Capitalism*. Westport: Quorum Books, 1994.

Klein, Naomi. *No Logo: Taking Aim at the Brand Bullies*. New York: St. Martin's Press, 1999.

Kuhn, Annette. *Powers of the Image: Essays on Representation and Sexuality*. New York and London: Routledge, 1985.

La Ferla, Ruth, "Wearing Their Beliefs on Their Chests," in *The New York Times*, March 29, 2005.

Lasch, Christopher. *The Culture of Narcissism: American Life in an Age of Diminishing Expectations*. New York: Norton, 1979.

Lasn, Kalle. *Culture Jam: The Uncooling of America*. New York: Eagle Brook, 1999.

Leach, William. *Land of Desire: Merchants, Power and the Rise of a New American Culture*. New York: Pantheon, 1993.

Lears, Jackson. *Fables of Abundance: A Cultural History of Advertising in America*. New York: Basic Books, 1994.

Lears, T.J. Jackson, "From Salvation to Self-Realization: Advertising and the Therapeutic Roots of the Consumer Culture, 1880–1930," in *The Culture of Consumption: Critical Essays in American History, 1880–1980*, ed. Richard Wightman Fox and T.J. Jackson Lears. New York: Pantheon Books, 1983.

Leiss, William et al. *Social Communication in Advertising: Persons, Products, and Images of Well-Being*. New York and London: Routledge, 1997.

Levi-Strauss, Claude. *Totemism*, trans. Rodney Needham. Boston: Beacon Press, 1962.

Lukes, Steven. *Emile Durkheim: His Life and Work: A Historical and Critical Study*. New York: Penguin Books, 1973.

Macquarrie, John. *Mediators between Human and Divine: From Moses to Muhammad*. New York: Continuum, 1996.

Maffesoli, Michael. *The Time of the Tribes: The Decline of Individualism in Mass Society*. London: Sage, 1996.

Marchand, Roland. *Advertising the American Dream: Making Way for Modernity, 1920–1940*. Berkeley: University of California Press, 1985.

Marx, Karl. *Capital*, Volume 1. Chicago: Charles H. Kerr & Company, 1912.

McCracken, Grant. *Culture and Consumption: New Approaches to the Symbolic Character of Consumer Goods and Activities*. Bloomington: Indiana University Press, 1988.

McDannell, Colleen. *Material Christianity: Religion and Popular Culture in America*. New Haven: Yale University Press, 1995.

McFague, Sallie. *Life Abundant: Rethinking Theology and Economy for a Planet in Peril*. Minneapolis: Fortress Press, 2001.

Meeks, M. Douglas. *God the Economist: The Doctrine of God and Political Economy*. Minneapolis: Fortress Press, 1989.

Melville, Stephen. "Division of the Gaze, or Remarks on the Color and Tenor of Contemporary 'Theory,' " in *Vision in Context: Historical and Contemporary Perspectives on Sight*, ed. Teresa Brennan and Martin Jay. New York and London: Routledge, 1996.

Moore, R. Laurence. *Selling God: American Religion in the Marketplace of Culture*. New York: Oxford University Press, 1994.

Neville, Robert Cummings. *Religion in Late Modernity*. Albany: State University of New York Press, 2002.

Packard, Vance. *The Hidden Persuaders*. New York: David McKay Company, Inc., 1957.

Pals, Daniel. *Seven Theories of Religion*. New York: Oxford University Press, 1996.

Pickering, W.S.F. *Durkheim's Sociology of Religion: Themes and Theories*. Boston: Routledge, 1984.

Poggi, Gianfranco. *Durkheim*. New York: Oxford University Press, 2000.

Proudfoot, Wayne. *Religious Experience*. Berkeley: University of California Press, 1985.

Sartre, Jean-Paul. *Being and Nothingness*, trans. Hazel E. Barnes. New York: Philosophical Library, 1956.

Sawicki, Jana. *Disciplining Foucault: Feminism, Power and the Body*. New York and London: Routledge, 1991.

Schmidt, Leigh Eric. *Consumer Rites: The Buying and Selling of American Holidays*. Princeton: Princeton University Press, 1995.

Schor, Juliet B. *The Overspent American: Why We Want What We Don't Need*. New York: HarperCollins, 1998.

Schor, Juliet B. and Douglas B. Holt. *The Consumer Society Reader*. New York: The New Press, 2000.

Schudson, Michael. *Advertising, the Uneasy Persuasion*. New York: Basic Books, 1984.

Sheffield, Tricia. "Advertising," in *Religion and American Cultures: An Encyclopedia of Traditions, Diversity, and Popular Expression*, Volume 2, ed. Gary Laderman and Luis Leon. Santa Barbara, CA: ABC-CLIO, 2003.

————. "Cover Girls: Toward a Theory of Female Divine Embodiment," in *The Journal of Religion and Society*, Volume 4, ed. Ronald Simkins. Omaha, Nebraska: Creighton University, 2002.

Sivulka, Juliann. *Soap, Sex, and Cigarettes: A Cultural History of American Advertising*. New York: Wadsworth Publishing Company, 1998.

Spencer, Baldwin and Francis James Gillen. *The Northern Tribes of Central Australia*. London: Macmillan, 1904.

————. *The Native Tribes of Central Australia*. London: Macmillan, 1899.

Spivak, Gayatri Chakravorty. "Can the Subaltern Speak?" in *Marxism and the Interpretation of Culture*, ed. Cary Nelson and Lawrence Grossberg. Urbana: University of Illinois Press, 1988.

Storey, John. *Cultural Consumption and Everyday Life*. London: Arnold Books, 1999.

Tanner, Katherine. *Theories of Culture: A New Agenda for Theology*. Minneapolis: Fortress Press, 1997.

Taylor, Mark C. *About Religion: Economies of Faith in Virtual Culture.* Chicago: The University of Chicago Press, 1999.

Taylor, Mark Kline. *Paul Tillich: Theologian of the Boundaries.* Minneapolis: Fortress Press, 1991.

———. *Remembering Esperanza: A Cultural–Political Theology for North American Praxis.* Maryknoll, NY: Orbis Books, 1990.

———. *Beyond Explanation: Religious Dimensions in Cultural Anthropology.* Macon, GA.: Mercer University Press, 1986.

Taylor, Mark McClain. "Tracking Spirit: Theology as Cultural Critique in the Americas," in *Changing Conversations: Religious Reflection and Cultural Analysis,* ed. Sheila Greeve Davaney and Dwight N. Hopkins. New York and London: Routledge, 1997.

Tillich, Paul. *Theology of Culture,* ed. Robert C. Kimball. New York and Oxford: Oxford University Press, 1964.

———. *Systematic Theology,* Volume 3. Chicago: The University of Chicago Press, 1963.

———. *Systematic Theology,* Volume 2. Chicago: The University of Chicago Press, 1957.

———. *Systematic Theology,* Volume 1. Chicago: The University of Chicago Press, 1951.

Twitchell, James. *Lead Us Into Temptation: The Triumph of American Materialism.* New York: Columbia University Press, 1999.

———. *ADCULT USA: The Triumph of Advertising in American Culture.* New York: Columbia University Press, 1996.

Tylor, Edward Burnett. *Primitive Culture.* London: J. Murray, 1871.

Veblen, Thorstein. *The Theory of the Leisure Class.* New York: Penguin, 1979.

Williamson, Judith. *Decoding Advertisements: Ideology and Meaning in Advertising.* London: Marion Boyars, 1978.

Index